TWELFTH NIGHT

HARBRACE SHAKESPEARE

TWELFTH NIGHT

edited by
Mark Maitman and Ian Waldron

HARCOURT
BRACE
CANADA

Harcourt Brace & Company, Canada
Toronto • Orlando • San Diego • London • Sydney

Harbrace Shakespeare: Series Editor, Ken Roy

Canadian Cataloguing in Publication Data

Shakespeare, William, 1564–1616
  Twelfth night

(Harbrace Shakespeare)
For use in high schools.
ISBN 0-7747-1365-9

I. Maitman, Mark. II. Waldron, Ian. III. Title.
IV. Series.

PR2837.A2M3 1990   822.3'3   C90-093255-4

93 94 95 96 97   6 5 4 3 2

Illustrators: Marika and Laszlo Gal
Cover Illustrators: Marika and Laszlo Gal

Printed in Canada

Acknowledgments

The editor and publisher acknowledge the consultants listed below for their contributions to the development of this program:

Nancy Steinhauer
Student, University of Toronto, Toronto, Ontario

Robert Tistechok
English Teacher, Humberside Collegiate, Toronto Board of Education, Toronto, Ontario

Gwen Vineberg
English Department Head, Royal West Academy, The Protestant School Board of Greater Montreal, Montreal, Quebec

To the Reader

This edition of *Twelfth Night* has been designed to encourage your active participation in the dramatic experience of Shakespeare's play.

Before reading each scene in the play, you will have an opportunity to explore ideas, themes, or personal experiences similar to the ones you will read about. You might want to discuss your opinions in small groups or, perhaps, record your responses in a journal.

As you begin to read each scene, a brief note will provide you with an outline of events within the scene, freeing you to think about the characters, their concerns and personalities, their relationships, and their interaction.

The notes of explanation which accompany Shakespeare's script are intended to enhance your reading and enrich your enjoyment and understanding of the play. You will discover your own way of using them to your advantage. Be careful never to let them interfere with your experience of the play itself. You can always return to some of the longer historical notes after your first reading of each scene.

Each scene is followed by a set of activities related to its themes and problems. You might want to explore these activities after each scene, after a group of scenes, or at the end of each act. Whichever you decide, you will discover that many of these activities, as with the questions before each scene, call for group work and personal response.

Your study of the play will be more efficient and productive if you maintain an organized approach. With your teacher, decide on what this approach will be. It might include a notebook for answering general questions, a personal journal or reading log, a writing folder for recording creative explorations and compositions, or a director's log or script book.

Now that you have some idea about how the text will be presented in the pages that follow, you are ready to experience the play.

Getting Started

Although *Twelfth Night* is set in medieval times, the issues and concerns which Shakespeare develops in the play are surprisingly contemporary. As you read the play, you will want to think about events in your own life and situations in the modern world that reflect the themes and ideas of the play. You might even want to take some time before you actually begin the text of the play to discuss some of the questions in small groups and record in your journal some of your classmates' responses, particularly those you find interesting or thought-provoking. Another possibility is to record your own thoughts on these issues in a series of personal journal entries.

1. Much of our behaviour is determined or controlled by the expectations of others. In what ways do friends influence our behaviour? What is the influence of parents? brothers and sisters? teachers? society at large? How do these expectations differ for males and females?

2. What are the qualities of a good friend? What obligations and commitments are a part of true friendship? When do we need friends most? What kind of behaviour might be considered a betrayal of friendship?

3. What is true love? What is the value of the rituals and ceremonies of courtship? How often are the games and conventions of love mistaken for "the real thing"? How can the traditional roles of men and women make love relationships more difficult?

4. The ancient Greeks taught that "the middle way is safest and best." How do you interpret this proverb? How can unbalanced behaviour be dangerous or unhealthy? How can we find "the middle way"?

5. Everybody loves good fun, but sometimes joking or "fooling" can become unfunny. When does this happen? Why does humour at times become cruel and spiteful? When can humour be helpful and instructive to us?

Return to these questions and your answers as you study the text. You will find that they provide you with a focus for discussing and writing about the play.

Dramatis Personae:
Literally, these Latin words mean "Masks of the Play." In Greek and Roman times, actors wore masks. Today and in Shakespeare's day, the title simply means "Characters."

gentlemen attending on the Duke:
Valentine and Curio would be attendants of some education and culture, not "servants" in the common sense of the term.

steward:
a man employed on a large estate to manage the domestic concerns, oversee the other servants, and keep the accounts

officer:
police officer

Dramatis Personae

(Characters in the Play)

Duke Orsino, Duke (or Count) of Illyria

Valentine
Curio } gentlemen attending on the Duke

Viola (later disguised
  as Cesario)
Sebastian } twins shipwrecked separately on the coast of Illyria

A Sea Captain, the ship's captain who rescued Viola
Antonio, another sea captain, friend to Sebastian
Olivia, a rich countess of Illyria
Maria, Olivia's lady-in-waiting
Feste, Olivia's jester
Malvolio, steward of Olivia's household
Fabian, a member of Olivia's household
Sir Toby Belch, Olivia's uncle
Sir Andrew Aguecheek, Sir Toby's friend
A Priest
First Officer
Second Officer
Lords, Sailors, Musicians and other Attendants
Scene: a city in Illyria and the sea-coast near it

Act 1, Scene 1

In this scene . . .

Orsino, the Duke of Illyria, is fiercely in love with Olivia,
a rich countess of Illyria. However, he is informed
that she is mourning the death of her brother and
refuses to hear the Duke's vows of love.

1   *play on:* Duke Orsino is speaking to his court musicians.

2   *that:* so that; *surfeiting:* eating too much, or in this case, hearing too much

4   *strain:* melody; *fall:* cadence, conclusion of a musical phrase

5-6   *sweet sound,/That breathes:* the whispering of a gentle breeze

7   *Stealing:* moving slowly and gently (also taking the fragrance from the flowers)

9   *quick:* Orsino uses the word in all its meanings: alive, sharp, keen.

10-11   *notwithstanding thy . . . sea:* although love has as great a capacity as the sea

11   *nought:* nothing

12   *Of what . . . soe'er:* of whatever value

13   *falls into abatement and low price:* loses its value

14   *shapes:* fantasies; *fancy:* love

15   *it alone is high fantastical:* Love is the emotion that most stimulates the imagination.

17   *hart:* Note the pun on hart (deer) and heart.

19-23   *O, when . . . me:* Orsino compares himself to Actæon, a Greek youth who came upon the goddess Artemis bathing in a pond when he was out hunting. He gazed in wonder at her beauty until she caught him looking and transformed him into a stag. Actæon's own hounds then chased and killed him.

20   *Methought:* I thought; *purged:* cleansed; *pestilence:* disease

22   *fell:* fierce, bloodthirsty

23   *E'er:* ever

24   *So please . . . admitted:* I hate to have to tell you this, my lord, but I was not able to gain admittance.

26   *element:* sky; *till seven years' heat:* until seven summers have passed

27   *at ample view:* in full view; Olivia has vowed that she will not even leave her house during her mourning.

28   *cloistress:* nun (i.e., shut off from the world in a religious community)

Act 1, Scene 1

A room in the Duke's palace.

Enter Duke Orsino, Curio, and other Lords;
Musicians attending.

[handwritten: Key place + people.]

Duke: If music be the food of love, play on; *[handwritten: Wants it to grow bigger + Stronger.]*
Give me excess of it, that, surfeiting,
The appetite may sicken, and so die. *[handwritten: Wants to much / hears to much.]*
That strain again! it had a dying fall.
O, it came o'er my ear like the sweet sound,   5
That breathes upon a bank of violets,
Stealing and giving odour! Enough; no more.
'Tis not so sweet now as it was before.
O spirit of love! how quick and fresh art thou!
That, notwithstanding thy capacity   10
Receiveth as the sea, nought enters there,
Of what validity and pitch soe'er,
But falls into abatement and low price,
Even in a minute: so full of shapes is fancy,
That it alone is high fantastical.   15
Curio: Will you go hunt, my lord? *[handwritten: trying to lift spirits / cheer him up.]*
Duke: What, Curio?
Curio: The hart. *[handwritten: Deer]*
Duke: Why, so I do, the noblest that I have.   *[handwritten: — Fell in love with Olivia]*
O, when mine eyes did see Olivia first,   *[handwritten: — Felt like a deer being hunted by his own desire for her.]*
Methought she purged the air of pestilence!   20
[handwritten left margin: Will clear the air of sickness]
That instant was I turn'd into a hart;
And my desires, like fell and cruel hounds,
E'er since pursue me.
[*Enter Valentine.*]   How now! what news from her?
Valentine: So please my lord, I might not be admitted;
But from her handmaid do return this answer: 25
The element itself, till seven years' heat,   *[handwritten: — She won't show her face for 7 years because she is mourning for her brother]*
Shall not behold her face at ample view;
But, like a cloistress, she will veiled walk

30   *eye-offending brine:* salt tears (which sting or offend her eyes as they fall); *season:* preserve (with her tears)

31   *A brother's dead love:* her love for her dead brother

33   *of that fine frame:* of such excellent composition

35   *rich golden shaft:* Cupid, the Roman boy-god of love, had two kinds of arrows (*shafts*): the arrows with golden tips caused instant love, while those with leaden tips caused hatred or scorn.

36   *all affections else:* all other emotions (but love)

37   *liver, brain, and heart:* It was believed that the liver, the brain, and the heart were the containers or seats (thrones) of sexual passion, thought, and feeling, respectively.

39   *one self king:* single lord or ruler

41   *bowers:* arbours, summer-houses. (Here, Orsino seems to mean simply flowers.)

And water once a day her chamber round
With eye-offending brine: all this to season   30
A brother's dead love, which she would keep fresh
And lasting in her sad remembrance.
Duke: O, she that hath a heart of that fine frame
To pay this debt of love but to a brother,
How will she love, when the rich golden shaft   35
Hath kill'd the flock of all affections else
That live in her; when liver, brain, and heart,
These sovereign thrones, are all supplied, and fill'd
Her sweet perfections with one self king!
Away before me to sweet beds of flowers;   40
Love-thoughts lie rich when canopied with bowers.

[*Exeunt.*]

illusion of cupids work.

-If she could love her brother that much-how much could she love me? Probably lots.

Recap:

The duke wants olivia to love him so much. Curio tries to cheer him up by getting him to go hunting. Valentine comes in a says" she is mourning and will not love for 7 years." The Duke says that if she loves her dead brother that much, then he could wait for 7 years for her to love him even more.

Act 1, Scene 1: Activities

1. "If music be the food of love, play on . . ."
   The first line of this play is a very famous one. Why do
   you think many people find the comparison between
   music and love appropriate? What two or three songs
   or pieces of music evoke thoughts of love in you?
   Why do couples often have a song that they associate
   with their romance? Find out the special song or
   music of your parents or an older couple you know.
   Share your responses with a partner or in a small
   group.

2. If you were asked to provide the music for this scene,
   what would you choose? Consider music for a variety
   of productions of the play: a current version, a fifties
   or sixties version, a nineteenth-century version, or a
   Shakespearean version. Share your choices with a
   partner, explaining fully your reasons.

3. If you were a psychologist asked to comment on the
   character and behaviour of both Orsino and Olivia
   from this brief glimpse, how would you describe them?
   In what ways are their situations similar? How are
   their emotional responses alike? Would you consider
   their behaviour "healthy"? Record your observations
   in a journal which you can refer to and add to throughout
   your reading of the play. Use "First Impressions of
   Olivia and Orsino" as the title of this entry.

4. Look at the illustration on page 5. How well does it
   capture the mood or "feel" of this opening scene?
   What changes (if any) might you suggest to the artist?
   Give reasons for your suggestions. You may wish to
   prepare an alternative illustration for the scene or
   compose a descriptive paragraph which captures
   the atmosphere of the scene.

For the next scene . . .

Imagine yourself stranded alone in a strange and potentially dangerous place. What would you do first? How well would you cope in such a crisis?

Act 1, Scene 2

In this scene . . .

There has been a shipwreck off the coast of Illyria. Viola,
a young woman in her late teens, has been saved,
but there is no news about Sebastian, her twin brother.
As a stranger in Illyria, Viola decides to disguise
herself as a young man and seek employment in the
Duke's court.

4   *Elysium:* in classical mythology, the home of the blessed dead, a kind of heaven

5   *Perchance:* perhaps. (In the next line, the captain uses the word to mean by chance, or by good fortune.)

8   *chance:* possibility

9   *did split:* was wrecked

11   *driving:* drifting, driven by the seas

12   *provident:* intelligent (literally, thinking ahead)

14   *lived:* floated

15   *Arion:* a young Greek musician who leapt into the sea to escape a crew of seamen who were planning to rob him; he was carried to safety on the back of a dolphin

16   *hold acquaintance with:* maintain a friendship with (i.e., he did not sink)

18   *gold:* gold coins (money)

19-21 *unfoldeth to . . . him:* reinforces my hope that, like me, he may have escaped, a hope that your words seem to support

30   *very late:* quite recently

Scene 2

The sea-coast.

Enter Viola, a Captain, and Sailors.

Viola: What country, friends, is this?
Captain: This is Illyria, lady.
Viola: And what should I do in Illyria?
My brother he is in Elysium.
Perchance he is not drown'd. What think you, sailors?   5
Captain: It is perchance that you yourself were saved.
Viola: Oh, my poor brother! and so perchance may he be.
Captain: True, madam; and, to comfort you with chance,
Assure yourself, after our ship did split,
When you and those poor number saved with you   10
Hung on our driving boat, I saw your brother,
~~Most~~ provident in peril, bind himself,   *intelligent*
Courage and hope both teaching him the practice,   *ninksahead*
To a strong mast that lived upon the sea;
Where, like Arion on the dolphin's back,   15
I saw him hold acquaintance with the waves
So long as I could see.
Viola: For saying so, there's gold.
Mine own escape unfoldeth to my hope,
Whereto thy speech serves for authority,   20
The like of him. Know'st thou this country?
Captain: Ay, madam, well; for I was bred and born
Not three hours' travel from this very place.
Viola: Who governs here?
Captain: A noble Duke, in nature as in name.   25
Viola: What is his name?
Captain: Orsino.
Viola: Orsino! I have heard my father name him.
He was a bachelor then.
Captain: And so is now, or was so very late;   30
For but a month ago I went from hence,

32	*'twas fresh in murmur:* there was a new rumour
33	*prattle:* gossip
40-41	*abjured the . . . men:* swore not to associate with men or even to see them
41	*O that:* I wish that
42	*deliver'd:* revealed, made known
43-44	*Till I had . . . estate is:* until I had found an appropriate opportunity to disclose my situation and position
44	*compass:* arrange, bring about
45	*admit:* pay attention to, consider, pay heed to; *suit:* petition, request
46	*No, not the Duke's:* not even the Duke's
47	*There is . . . thee:* You appear to be an honest person.
48	*though that:* although
49	*oft:* often; *close in:* hide
50-51	*suits/With:* matches (literally, is appropriate to)
51	*character:* appearance
52	*I prithee:* I pray you, I ask you
53	*Conceal me what I am:* do not reveal who I am
54-55	*haply shall . . . intent:* will perhaps serve my purposes
56	*eunuch:* castrated male. Eunuchs were commonly used as tutors and servants in Elizabethan courts. Castration halts the development of facial hair and the natural lowering of the male voice in adolescence. Viola's high-pitched voice, therefore, would not arouse suspicion.
59	*allow me . . . service:* allow me to prove myself worthy to be one of his servants
60	*hap:* happen; *to time I will commit:* I will leave in the hands of time
61	*shape:* fit; *wit:* thinking, i.e., plan
62	*mute:* silent servant
63	*When my . . . see:* If I tell, may I be cursed and go blind.

And then 'twas fresh in murmur,—as, you know,
What great ones do the less will prattle of,— *gossip*
That he did seek the love of fair Olivia.
Viola: What's she?   35
Captain: A virtuous maid, the daughter of a count
That died some twelvemonths since; then leaving her
In the protection of his son, her brother,
Who shortly also died: for whose dear love,
They say, she hath abjured the company   40
And sight of men.
Viola: O that I served that lady,
And might not be deliver'd to the world,
Till I had made mine own occasion mellow,
What my estate is!
Captain: That were hard to compass,
Because she will admit no kind of suit,   45
No, not the Duke's.   *Beautiful*
Viola: There is a fair behaviour in thee, captain; *looks may be*
And though that nature with a beauteous wall *deseaving yet her*
Doth oft close in pollution, yet of thee *instincts tell her she is*
I will believe thou hast a mind that suits *a good man?*
With this thy fair and outward character.
I prithee, and I'll pay thee bounteously,
Conceal me what I am, and be my aid
For such disguise as haply shall become
a guy who The form of my intent. I'll serve this Duke;   55
lost his Thou shalt present me as an eunuch to him.
It may be worth thy pains; for I can sing
And speak to him in many sorts of music,
That will allow me very worth his service.
What else may hap to time I will commit;   60
Only shape thou thy silence to my wit.
Captain: Be you his eunuch, and your mute I'll be.
When my tongue blabs, then let mine eyes not see.
Viola: I thank thee; lead me on.   [*Exeunt.*]

Act 1, Scene 2: Activities

1. Imagine that you are directing this scene and have decided to use a bare stage. You don't have any painted backdrops to suggest outdoor scenery, and you can't use sets to suggest walls, doors, windows, and so on. How do you show the audience that the scene takes place outdoors, at the sea coast? You might think of using costumes, props, sound effects, lighting, and special effects.

   Brainstorm some ideas in a group and share them with the class. In a director's log, summarize strategies for creating the appropriate setting that you think would work most effectively.

2. How is Viola's response to her "crisis" different from that of Orsino and Olivia in the previous scene? Compile a list of words and phrases which describe the Viola you meet in this scene.

   Make additions and changes to this list as you learn more about Viola in the coming scenes.

3. a) Why would Viola decide to disguise herself as a young man while she is in Illyria? What uncertainties would she face as a woman alone in a strange land? In the role of Viola, compose a diary entry in which you reflect upon these problems.

   b) How might a modern woman cope in a similar situation? Rewrite this scene with Viola as a contemporary heroine.

For the next scene . . .

What are some unwritten rules that govern your behaviour when you are a guest in the home of a friend or relative? What consequences might you expect if you broke these rules?

Act 1, Scene 3

In this scene . . .

Sir Toby Belch, a relative of Olivia, has moved into her house. His rowdy behaviour is disturbing the entire household. Maria, Olivia's lady-in-waiting, warns Sir Toby that his actions will get him into trouble, but he seems determined to take advantage of Olivia's hospitality. Toby is joined by his friend, Sir Andrew Aguecheek, who has decided not to pursue his courtship of Olivia any further. Toby encourages Sir Andrew not to give up so easily, and the two drink into the night.

1   *What a plague:* what the devil; *niece:* It is unlikely that Sir Toby is Olivia's uncle. He seems to use the term in a more general sense to mean a young female relative.

3   *By my troth:* to tell the truth

4-5   *takes great exceptions/to:* objects very strongly to

5   *ill:* irregular

6   *except:* make formal objections. Sir Toby parodies the jargon of the legal profession.

7-8   *confine yourself . . . order:* restrict yourself within the limits of good behaviour. (In line 9, Sir Toby puns on *confine* in the sense of "dress.")

11   *An:* if

13   *quaffing:* heavy drinking; *undo:* ruin (i.e., Olivia will break her connections with you.)

18   *tall:* In Elizabethan England, this description often implied bravery and boldness, but Sir Toby may simply be referring to Sir Andrew's height.

21   *ducats:* gold coins

22   *prodigal:* a wasteful person

23   *Fie:* expression of disgust or outrage (damn it!)

23-24   *viol-de-/gamboys:* a stringed instrument like a cello. (Sir Toby's bad French is an attempt at the Italian term *viola da gamba*, a fiddle held between the knees.)

25   *without book:* by heart. (Sir Andrew can recite passages from memory, but probably does not understand their meaning.)

27   *almost natural:* Sir Andrew is a natural fool, a "born idiot."

29   *allay:* soften, counterbalance; *gust:* gusto, flourish

31   *have the gift of a grave:* be given a grave, be killed

Scene 3

words not wonderful

A room in Olivia's house.

Enter Sir Toby Belch and Maria.

Sir Toby = relative of Olivia.

Not very smart

Sir Toby: What a plague means my niece, to take the death
of her brother thus? I am sure care's an enemy to life.

Maria: By my troth, Sir Toby, you must come in earlier
o' nights. Your cousin, my lady, takes great exceptions
to your ill hours.   5

Sir Toby: Why, let her except, before excepted.

Maria: Ay, but you must confine yourself within the modest
limits of order.

Sir Toby: Confine! I'll confine myself no finer than I am.
These clothes are good enough to drink in; and so be   10
these boots too. An they be not, let them hang themselves in their own straps.

Heavy drinking

Maria: That quaffing and drinking will undo you. I heard
my lady talk of it yesterday; and of a foolish knight *romancer.*
that you brought in one night here to be her wooer.   15

Sir Toby: Who, Sir Andrew Aguecheek?

Maria: Ay, he.

Sir Toby: He's as tall a man as any's in Illyria.

Maria: What's that to the purpose?

Sir Toby: Why, he has three thousand ducats a year.   20

gold coins

Maria: Ay, but he'll have but a year in all these ducats;
he's a very fool and a prodigal. *Wasteful person*

Sir Toby: Fie, that you'll say so! He plays o' the viol-de-
gamboys, and speaks three or four languages word for
word without book, and hath all the good gifts of   25
nature. *Naturally born an idiot*

like a cello.

Speaks many languages well!

Maria: He hath indeed, almost natural: for besides that he's
a fool, he's a great quarreller; and but that he hath
the gift of a coward to allay the gust he hath in quar-
relling, 'tis thought among the prudent he would   30
quickly have the gift of a grave.

He is alive, because when he challenged he becomes a fool and doesn't fight. He gets away with H.

32	*substractors:* Sir Toby's mistaken way of saying "detractors."
38	*coystrill:* villain (literally, a groom who takes care of a knight's horses)
39	*turn o' the toe:* spin. (Compare it with the modern word "topsy-turvy.")
40	*parish-top:* In many Elizabethan towns and villages, a large top was available for exercise and entertainment. Presumably the villagers would whip or spin the top in frosty weather, keeping warm from the exercise and out of mischief when they were out of work; *Castiliano vulgo:* It is not clear what Sir Toby means. Perhaps Sir Toby is advising Maria to treat Sir Andrew with more polite respect. The Castilians (from Castille, in Spain) were noted for their stiff formality; *Agueface:* Like Aguecheek, the name suggests the sickly and pale complexion of a person suffering from an *ague* or fever.
44	*shrew:* a small mouse-like animal.
46	*Accost:* greet her, speak to her
48	*chambermaid:* lady-in-waiting, companion (not a servant who performs menial taks)
53	*front:* confront, approach directly; *board:* greet, approach (as one boards a ship)
55	*undertake:* tackle. (Sir Andrew has clearly understood the sexual meaning of Sir Toby's commands.)
58	*An thou let part so:* if you let her go
61-62	*do you . . . hand:* Do you think you are dealing with fools? (Maria's reply uses "hand" in the literal sense.)
64	*Marry:* a mild oath ("by the Virgin Mary")
65	*"thought is free":* I may think what I like.
66	*buttery-bar:* A buttery is a store-room for wine and liquor. Drinkers would sit their jugs on the ledge (or "bar") at the doorway of the buttery. Most directors have Maria place Sir Andrew's hand on her breast as she speaks this line.
68	*dry:* thirsty (also "barren" or "sexless"; a moist palm was a sign of sexual arousal)
69-70	*I am not . . . dry:* Sir Andrew misses Maria's joke. Shakespeare is playing with the proverb, "Fools have wit enough to keep themselves out of the rain."

Sir Toby: By this hand, they are scoundrels and substractors ~~Ditractors~~

that say so of him. Who are they?

Maria: They that add, moreover, he's drunk nightly in your

company. 35

Sir Toby: With drinking healths to my niece. I'll drink to

her as long as there is a passage in my throat and *takes care of*

drink in Illyria. He's a coward and a coystrill that will *knights horses*

not drink to my niece till his brains turn o' the toe

~~Exercise~~like a parish-top. What, wench! Castiliano vulgo! For 40

~~equipment~~there comes Sir Andrew Agueface. *Polite respect*

[*Enter Sir Andrew Aguecheek.*]

Sir Andrew: Sir Toby Belch! How now, Sir Toby Belch!

Sir Toby: Sweet Sir Andrew!

Sir Andrew: Bless you, fair shrew. *small mouse like animal*

Maria: And you too, sir. 45

Sir Toby: Accost, Sir Andrew, accost.

Sir Andrew: What's that?

Sir Toby: My niece's chambermaid. *lady in waiting*

Sir Andrew: Good Mistress Accost, I desire better

acquaintance. 50

Maria: My name is Mary, sir.

Sir Andrew: Good Mistress Mary Accost,—

Sir Toby: You mistake, knight: "accost" is front her, board

her, woo her, assail her. *Food dish*

food dish *Sir Andrew:* By my troth, I would not undertake her in this 55

company. Is that the meaning of "accost"?

Maria: Fare you well, gentlemen.

Sir Toby: An thou let part so, Sir Andrew, would thou

mightst never draw sword again.

Sir Andrew: An you part so, mistress, I would I might never 60

draw sword again. Fair lady, do you think you have

fools in hand?

Maria: Sir, I have not you by the hand.

Sir Andrew: Marry, but you shall have; and here's my hand.

Maria: Now, sir, "thought is free". I pray you, bring your 65

hand to the buttery-bar and let it drink. *Wine room bar*

Sir Andrew: Wherefore, sweetheart? What's your metaphor?

Maria: It's dry, sir.

Sir Andrew: Why, I think so. I am not such an ass but I

can keep my hand dry. But what's your jest? 70

71   *dry:* ironic or wry, and also dull or barren (since Sir Andrew did not catch the joke)

73   *at my fingers' ends:* at the ready

74   *barren:* dull-witted, without any more jokes

75   *thou lackest a cup of canary:* You need a drink (wine from the Canary Islands).

76   *put down:* either dejected (by his lack of success with Olivia) or defeated (by Maria's superior wit)

78   *put me down:* make me drunk

80   *beef:* It was a common Elizabethan belief that eating too much beef would dull the brain.

83   *forswear:* give up

87   *tongues:* languages. Sir Toby's response in line 90 is based upon the punning of "tongues" and "tongs" (curling irons).

91   *mended:* improved

92   *Past question:* without a doubt

94   *becomes:* suits

95-97 *it hangs . . . off:* Toby's joke depends on a complex set of comparisons. Andrew's hair is like *flax*, a pale yellow fibre that was wound on to a cleft stick called a *distaff*. Women would customarily hold the distaff between their legs as they worked with the spinning wheel to produce linen. The term *housewife* was often used to mean prostitute. Contact with such a woman would give Sir Andrew syphilis and cause all his hair to fall out.

99-100 *she'll/none of me:* She is not interested in me.

100   *hard by:* very near here

101   *match:* marry

102   *degree:* social position; *estate:* wealth

103   *there's life in't:* There's hope in your suit.

105   *masques:* parties at which the guests wore masks

107   *kickshawses:* trifles (French: *quelques choses*)

108-109 *under/the degree of my betters:* beneath the rank of my social superiors (i.e., "I am as good as anyone who is not better than me!")

Maria: A dry jest, sir.

Sir Andrew: Are you full of them?

Maria: Ay, sir, I have them at my fingers' ends. Marry,
now I let go your hand, I am barren.   [*Exit.*]

Sir Toby: O knight, thou lackest a cup of canary. When   75
did I see thee so put down?

you need a drink

Sir Andrew: Never in your life, I think, unless you see canary
put me down. Methinks sometimes I have no more
wit than a Christian or an ordinary man has; but I am
a great eater of beef, and I believe that does harm to   80
my wit.

Sir Toby: No question.

give up

Sir Andrew: An I thought that, I'd forswear it. I'll ride home
to-morrow, Sir Toby.

Sir Toby: Pourquoi, my dear knight?   *he should know how to speak french*

Sir Andrew: What is "pourquoi"? Do or not do? I would I
had bestowed that time in the tongues that I have
in fencing, dancing, and bear-baiting. O, had I but
followed the arts!

Sir Toby: Then hadst thou had an excellent head of hair.   90

Sir Andrew: Why, would that have mended my hair?   *improved*

Sir Toby: Past question, for thou seest it will not curl by
nature. *without a doubt*

Sir Andrew: But it becomes me well enough, does't not?   *cleft stick*

Sir Toby: Excellent; it hangs like flax on a distaff and I hope   95
to see a housewife take thee between her legs, and
spin it off.

yellow fiber

Sir Andrew: Faith, I'll home to-morrow, Sir Toby. Your
niece will not be seen; or if she be, it's four to one she'll
none of me. The count himself here hard by woos her.   100

He doesn't think she'll go out with him

Sir Toby: She'll none o' the count. She'll not match above
her degree, neither in estate, years, nor wit. I have
heard her swear't. Tut, there's life in't, man.

there is hope in your suit.

Sir Andrew: I'll stay a month longer. I am a fellow o' the
strangest mind i' the world; I delight in masques and   105
revels sometimes altogether.

party masks,

Sir Toby: Art thou good at these kickshawses, knight?   *Trifles.*

Sir Andrew: As any man in Illyria, whatsoever he be, under
the degree of my betters; and yet I will not compare
with an old man.   110

29

111   *galliard:* quick and lively dance

112   *cut a caper:* perform the leap in a galliard. (Sir Toby's following line puns on another meaning of "caper" – a pickled berry eaten with meat.)

114   *back-trick:* probably some sort of reverse step in dancing

116-117 *Wherefore have/ . . . before 'em?:* Why are you hiding these talents? Curtains were hung in front of paintings to protect them from light and dust.

118   *Mistress Mall's:* The allusion here is not clear.

120   *coranto:* lively running dance; *jig:* lively jumping dance

123   *under a star of a galliard:* Sir Andrew seems to have been born when the stars favoured dancing. Horoscopes were as popular in Elizabethan times as in modern times.

124   *does indifferent well:* does well enough

125   *stock:* stocking

127-128 *born under/Taurus?:* born between April 20 and May 20, the sign of the Bull. Each sign of the zodiac was related to a different part of the body. Toby and Andrew do not seem to know their astrology very well. Taurus was usually associated with the neck and throat.

Sir Toby: What is thy excellence in a galliard, knight? *quick and lively*

Sir Andrew: Faith, I can cut a caper. *leap in a galliard.* *dance*

Sir Toby: And I can cut the mutton to't.

Sir Andrew: And I think I have the back-trick simply as
    strong as any man in Illyria.   115

Sir Toby: Wherefore are these things hid? Wherefore have
    these gifts a curtain before 'em? Are they like to take
    dust, like Mistress Mall's picture? Why dost thou not
    go to church in a galliard and come home in a
    coranto? My very walk should be a jig. What dost thou 120
    mean? Is it a world to hide virtues in? I did think,
    by the excellent constitution of thy leg, it was formed
    under a star of a galliard.

Sir Andrew: Ay, 'tis strong, and it does indifferent well in
    a flame-coloured stock. Shall we set about some 125
    revels?   *Stockings –*

Sir Toby: What shall we do else? Were we not born under
    Taurus?

Sir Andrew: Taurus! That's sides and heart.

Sir Toby: No, sir; it is legs and thighs. Let me see thee 130
    caper. Ha! higher; ha, ha! excellent!   *[Exeunt.]*

sir andrew was born when the stars favoured dancing

Act 1, Scene 3: Activities

1. This is the last of the introductory scenes. What does it tell you about Toby, Andrew, and Maria? With a partner or in a small group, decide
   • whether you like these characters
   • whether you approve of them
   • what features of their conversation or behaviour might be offensive to some
   Compare your conclusions with those of another pair or group.

2. In a group of two or three, choose a short section of this scene and prepare it for dramatic presentation to the class. Emphasize both the verbal humour (puns and nonsense) and the physical humour (facial expressions, actions, and gestures). Ask the audience to respond to your dramatization and to suggest ways of making the scene even funnier.

3. In a small group reread the scene carefully in order to discover the characteristics of low comedy. Pay particular attention to the antics and jokes which are suggested in the dialogue. In your own words, define low comedy. To extend your definition, consider contemporary comedians/actors who use similar techniques.

4. Keeping in mind the unusual personality of Sir Andrew, compose a love letter to Olivia in which you, as Andrew, convince her to consider you as a suitor.

For the next scene . . .

How would you feel if a friend asked you to arrange a date with someone else? Suppose you yourself were attracted to your friend. How might your own attraction complicate the situation?

Act 1, Scene 4

In this scene . . .

Viola, disguised as a young male servant by the name of Cesario, is working for Orsino. He has quickly developed a deep affection for Cesario and has described to him his feelings for Olivia. Orsino sends Cesario to Olivia with his message of love. Meanwhile, Viola herself falls in love with Orsino.

2 *much advanced:* promoted

3 *but:* only

5 *humour:* personality; here, Orsino's unsteady disposition or whims; *negligence:* neglect of duty

11 *On your attendance:* at your service

12 *aloof:* aside

13 *no less but all:* everything; *unclasp'd:* revealed, opened

15 *address thy gait:* direct your steps

16 *access:* entry

17 *fixed:* determined, unshakeable, planted (as a tree)

18 *audience:* attention

21 *Be clamorous . . . bounds:* Shout, and ignore all the rules of reasonable behaviour.

22 *unprofited:* unsuccessful

24 *unfold:* reveal in detail

25 *Surprise:* make a sudden attack, take by storm; *dear:* intense

26 *become:* suit

27 *attend:* hear, listen to

28 *nuncio's:* messenger's; *grave aspect:* serious appearance

[handwritten: Poetry important / Paragraph unimportant]

Scene 4

[handwritten: word not understood / important parts]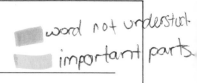

Duke Orsino's palace.

Enter Valentine, and Viola in man's attire.

[handwritten: Exaggeration for effect: Hyperbole — / Starts with a paragraph then poetry.]

Valentine: If the duke continue these favours towards you,
Cesario, you are like to be much advanced. He hath
known you but three days, and already you are no
stranger.

Viola: You either fear his humour or my negligence, that   5
you call in question the continuance of his love. Is he
inconstant, sir, in his favours?

Valentine: No, believe me.

Viola: I thank you. Here comes the count.
[*Enter Duke, Curio, and Attendants.*]

Duke: Who saw Cesario, ho?   10

Viola: On your attendance, my lord; here.

Duke: Stand you a while aloof. Cesario,   *[handwritten: aside]*
Thou know'st no less but all. I have unclasp'd
To thee the book even of my secret soul;
Therefore, good youth, address thy gait unto her;   *[handwritten: Direct your steps]* 15
Be not denied access, stand at her doors,
And tell them, there thy fixed foot shall grow
Till thou have audience.

Viola: Sure, my noble lord,
If she be so abandon'd to her sorrow
As it is spoke, she never will admit me.   20

Duke: Be clamorous and leap all civil bounds   *[handwritten: Ignore rules of good behaviour]*
Rather than make unprofited return.

Viola: Say I do speak with her, my lord, what then?

Duke: Oh, then unfold the passion of my love,
Surprise her with discourse of my dear faith *[handwritten: Suit]*   25
It shall become thee well to act my woes;
She will attend it better in thy youth
Than in a nuncio's of more grave aspect.

[handwritten: Messenger's.]   *[handwritten: Serious appearance]*

30   *belie:* give a false impression of

31   *Diana's lip:* the beautiful Roman goddess of the moon, the
      hunt, and spiritual love

32   *rubious:* ruby red; *pipe:* voice

33   *organ:* organ of speech, voice; *shrill and sound:* high-pitched
      and clear

34   *semblative:* like; *part:* nature

35   *constellation:* personality (as determined by the position of the
      stars at her birth); *right apt:* very suitable

38   *When least in company:* alone

41   *barful strife:* dilemma full of obstacles (or bars)

Viola: I think not so, my lord.   [Give a false impression]

Duke: Dear lad, believe it;
  For they shall yet belie thy happy years,
  That say thou art a man. Diana's lip   [Goddess of spiritual love.]   30
  Is not more smooth and rubious; thy small pipe
  Is as the maiden's organ, shrill and sound;
  [Part]   And all is semblative a woman's part.
  [Nature]   I know thy constellation is right apt   [Dramatic
  For this affair. Some four or five attend him,   Irony]   35
  All, if you will; for I myself am best
  When least in company. Prosper well in this,
  And thou shalt live as freely as thy lord,
  To call his fortunes thine.
Viola: I'll do my best
  To woo your lady; [*Aside.*] yet, a barful strife!   [Dilemma full of   40
  Whoe'er I woo, myself would be his wife.   [*Exeunt.*]   obstacles]

Thinking out
loud.

We must take to the theatre that
willing suspension of disbelief that
constitutes poetic faith
= Use your imagination of
disbelief.
- Go along with your instincts.
                    (the game)

Act 1, Scene 4: Activities

1. Orsino gives Cesario a difficult task – to court a woman who will have nothing to do with him. As Viola, what tricks or gimmicks might you use to get Olivia's attention? What arguments might you use to convince Olivia to meet with Orsino?

   Write a speech that would gain Olivia's sympathy and agreement. You might rehearse the speech for presentation to a group or to the class.

2. Orsino is adhering to an Elizabethan courtship ritual by sending his servant to speak on his behalf. How would he attract Olivia's attention in today's society? (He might, for example, send a singing telegram, or hire an advertising agency.) Make a list of all the possibilities. Use your imagination!

   For fun, find out how someone of your parents' or grandparents' generation would have acted in this situation.

3. Dramatic irony occurs when the audience knows something of which some or all of the characters on stage are unaware. In this scene, there is dramatic irony in Orsino's praise of Cesario's "feminine" qualities. Find another example in this scene. In a small group, predict what other ironic situations may develop as a result of Viola's disguise.

For the next scene . . .

What makes people fall in love? Do you believe in "love at first sight"? Why or why not?

Act 1, Scene 5

In this scene . . .

Maria is scolding Feste for his absence from the house, when Olivia enters. She is with her steward, Malvolio. Since Olivia is still depressed over the death of her brother, Feste tries to amuse her. When Malvolio reveals his contempt for Feste's good humour, Olivia defends the fool and criticizes Malvolio's sour personality. Cesario (Viola) arrives as Orsino's messenger, but is prevented from entering the house by the drunken Sir Toby. Malvolio is sent to remove Viola from the premises, but her stubborn determination arouses Olivia's curiosity and she decides to see the messenger. Viola delivers an eloquent description of Orsino's love, but Olivia isn't convinced. Instead she is attracted to Cesario, not realizing that "he" is a "she." Although she rejects Orsino's message, she sends Malvolio after Cesario, once he has departed, to give back a ring that she claims he forced upon her. The ring, of course, does not belong to Cesario: Olivia just wants to ensure that Cesario will return.

2-3   *in/way of thy excuse:* to provide an excuse for you

6   *fear no colours:* fear nothing (with a pun on *colour* – military flag and *collar* – hangman's noose)

7   *Make that good:* Explain what you mean.

9   *lenten:* plain. (During the forty days of Lent leading up to Easter, Christians are supposed to eat only the plainest foods.)

12   *In the wars:* on the battlefield, i.e., in trouble

12-13   *and that . . . foolery:* Maria's answer suggests that Feste would be bold indeed to tell his mistress, Olivia, that he does not fear her wrath or displeasure.

15   *talents:* native intelligence

17   *turned away:* dismissed, fired

20   *for:* as for; *let summer bear it out:* Summer is a good time to be fired because the weather is warm.

21   *You are resolute, then?:* You refuse to explain your meaning?

22   *points:* matters. Maria's response plays on *points* as laces or suspenders to hold up Feste's pants.

24   *gaskins:* breeches, wide pants

26-27   *piece/of Eve's flesh:* woman. (Feste's compliment is ironic, for Sir Toby is most unlikely to give up drinking. Feste may also be suggesting a match between Sir Toby and Maria.)

29   *you were best:* it would be best for you

Scene 5

Olivia's house.

Enter Maria and Feste.

Maria: Nay, either tell me where thou hast been, or I will
   not open my lips so wide as a bristle may enter in
   way of thy excuse. My lady will hang thee for thy
   absence.

Feste: Let her hang me; he that is well hanged in this world   5
   needs to fear no colours.

Maria: Make that good.

Feste: He shall see none to fear.

Maria: A good lenten answer. I can tell thee where that
   saying was born, of "I fear no colours".   10

Feste: Where, good Mistress Mary?

Maria: In the wars; and that may you be bold to say in your
   foolery.

Feste: Well, God give them wisdom that have it; and those
   that are fools, let them use their talents.   15

Maria: Yet you will be hanged for being so long absent;
   or, to be turned away, is not that as good as a hanging
   to you?

Feste: Many a good hanging prevents a bad marriage; and,
   for turning away, let summer bear it out.   20

Maria: You are resolute, then?

Feste: Not so, neither; but I am resolved on two points.

Maria: That if one break, the other will hold; or, if both
   break, your gaskins fall.

Feste: Apt, in good faith, very apt. Well, go thy way; if Sir   25
   Toby would leave drinking, thou wert as witty a piece
   of Eve's flesh as any in Illyria.

Maria: Peace, you rogue, no more o' that. Here comes my
   lady. Make your excuse wisely, you were best. [*Exit.*]

43

30   *an't:* if it.

32   *pass for:* be considered

33   *Quinapalus?:* No such person exists. Feste has invented an authority to support his own views.

38   *Go to:* stop, enough; *dry:* dull, witless

39   *dishonest:* disobedient, unreliable

40   *madonna:* my lady; *counsel:* advice

42   *dry:* thirsty; *bid:* ask

44   *botcher:* tailor (who mends old clothes with patches)

47   *syllogism:* logical argument; *serve:* prove useful; *so:* that's fine

47-48   *what/remedy?:* so what

48   *cuckold:* Olivia has married calamity, but she will not be faithful to it when she realizes that the days of beauty and youth are short and must be lived when she may do so.

49   *bade:* ordered

52   *Misprision:* misunderstanding, ignorance

52-53   *cucullus non/facit monachum:* A monk's hood does not make a monk. In the same way, Feste is not necessarily a fool just because he wears the costume of a fool or court jester.

54   *motley:* clothing mended with patches of many colours (the traditional costume of a court jester)

57   *Dexteriously:* dextrously, skilfully

59   *catechize you:* ask you questions

59-60   *Good my mouse/of virtue:* my good and virtuous mouse (used to show affection for Olivia)

61   *idleness:* amusement, entertainment; *bide:* wait. (Compare to the modern expression "to bide one's time.")

Feste: Wit, an't be thy will, put me into good fooling! 30
    Those wits, that think they have thee, do very oft prove
    fools; and I, that am sure I lack thee, may pass for a
    wise man. For what says Quinapalus? "Better a witty
    fool than a foolish wit." *(Made up person)*
    [*Enter Lady Olivia with Malvolio.*]
    God bless thee, lady! 35
Olivia: Take the fool away.
Feste: Do you not hear, fellows? Take away the lady.
Olivia: Go to, you're a dry fool; I'll no more of you. Besides,
    you grow dishonest. *(My lady)*
Feste: Two faults, madonna, that drink and good counsel 40
    will amend: for give the dry fool drink, then is the
    fool not dry; bid the dishonest man mend himself; if
    he mend, he is no longer dishonest; if he cannot, let the
    botcher mend him. Anything that's mended is but
    patched: virtue that transgresses is but patched with sin; 45
    and sin that amends is but patched with virtue. If that
    this simple syllogism will serve, so; if it will not, what *(logical argument)*
    remedy? As there is no true cuckold but calamity, so
    beauty's a flower. The lady bade take away the fool;
    therefore, I say again, take her away. *(not a fool because he is 50)*
Olivia: Sir, I bade them take away you. *(dressed like one.)*
Feste: Misprision in the highest degree! Lady, cucullus non *(mis- understood)*
    facit monachum. That's as much to say as I wear not
    motley in my brain. Good madonna, give me leave
    to prove you a fool. 55
Olivia: Can you do it?
Feste: Dexteriously, good madonna.
Olivia: Make your proof. *(Ask questions)*
Feste: I must catechize you for it, madonna. Good my mouse
    of virtue, answer me. 60
Olivia: Well, sir, for want of other idleness, I'll bide your
    proof.
Feste: Good madonna, why mournest thou?
Olivia: Good fool, for my brother's death.
Feste: I think his soul is in hell, madonna. 65
Olivia: I know his soul is in heaven, fool.
Feste: The more fool, madonna, to mourn for your brother's
    soul being in heaven. Take away the fool, gentlemen.

70   *mend?:* improve, get better. (Malvolio takes "mend" to mean "become more and more a fool.")

72   *Infirmity:* the weakness that comes with old age

75   *be sworn:* take an oath

76   *no fox:* not clever. (The Elizabethans considered the fox to be the most cunning and clever of animals); *pass his word:* be bribed

80   *barren:* lacking in wit; *put down:* defeated. (The expression has been revived in modern slang.)

82   *out of his guard:* defenceless. (The opposite, in the sport of fencing, is "on guard.")

83   *minister occasion:* provide him with opportunities

84   *protest:* declare; *crow so:* laugh so loudly and boisterously

85   *set:* dull, unoriginal; *zanies:* assistants, "straight men"

87   *distempered:* sick; *generous:* liberal-minded

88   *of free disposition:* good-natured

88-89 *bird-/bolts:* blunt arrows for shooting small birds

90   *allowed:* licensed (to speak freely); *rail:* mock

91   *known discreet man:* man of good judgement

93   *Now Mercury . . . leasing:* May Mercury make you a skilled liar. Mercury was the Roman god of liars, cheats, tricksters, and thieves.

98   *fair:* good-looking

98-99 *well/attended:* accompanied by many servants

100   *hold him in delay?:* are making him wait at the door

103   *madman:* the words of a madman

104   *suit:* petition, request

106   *old:* tiresome, tedious

Olivia: What think you of this fool, Malvolio? doth he not
    mend? 70
Malvolio: Yes, and shall do till the pangs of death shake
    him. Infirmity, that decays the wise, doth ever make
    the better fool.
Feste: God send you, sir, a speedy infirmity, for the better
    increasing your folly! Sir Toby will be sworn that I 75
    am no fox; but he will not pass his word for two pence
    that you are no fool.
Olivia: How say you to that, Malvolio?
Malvolio: I marvel your ladyship takes delight in such a
    barren rascal. I saw him put down the other day with 80
    an ordinary fool that has no more brain than a stone.
    Look you now, he's out of his guard already. Unless
    you laugh and minister occasion to him, he is gagged.
    I protest, I take these wise men, that crow so at these
    set kind of fools, no better than the fools' zanies. — *Assistance* 85
Olivia: O, you are sick of self-love, Malvolio, and taste with *"straight*
    a distempered appetite. To be generous, guiltless, and *men!"*
    of free disposition, is to take those things for bird-
    bolts that you deem cannon-bullets. There is no slander
    in an allowed fool, though he do nothing but rail; nor 90
    no railing in a known discreet man, though he do
    nothing but reprove.
Feste: Now Mercury endue thee with leasing, for thou
    speakest well of fools!
    [*Re-enter Maria.*]
Maria: Madam, there is at the gate a young gentleman much 95
    desires to speak with you.
Olivia: From the Count Orsino, is it?
Maria: I know not, madam; 'tis a fair young man, and well
    attended. *Accompanied by many servants.*
Olivia: Who of my people hold him in delay? 100
Maria: Sir Toby, madam, your kinsman.
Olivia: Fetch him off, I pray you; he speaks nothing but
    words of madman; fie on him! [*Exit Maria.*] Go you, Malvolio.
    madman, If it be a suit from the count, I am sick, or not at
    home—what you will, to dismiss it. [*Exit Malvolio.*] 105
    Now you see, sir, how your fooling grows old, and
    people dislike it.

108 *for us:* on our behalf, in defence of fools

109 *Jove:* Jupiter, the chief god of Romans

111 *pia mater:* brain

116 *a plague o':* a curse on. (Toby pretends that pickled herrings, rather than liquor, are making him belch.)

117 *sot:* fool

120 *lethargy?:* drowsiness, laziness

121 *I defy lechery:* I depise lechery. Toby's drunkenness has affected his hearing.

123 *an:* if

123-124 *Give/me faith:* Toby needs faith to resist the devil at the door.

127 *draught:* draft, drink; *above heat:* beyond what is necessary to maintain a person's normal body temperature; *mads:* makes him mad

129 *crowner:* coroner (in this case, a doctor who issues official certificates of death)

129-130 *sit o'/my coz:* hold an inquiry into the death of my kinsman to figure out what killed him

135-136 *he takes . . . much:* he says that he knows this

140 *fortified:* armed and able to resist

142 *Has:* he has

143 *sheriff's post:* a post set up outside the sheriff's door for notices and proclamations

Feste: Thou hast spoke for us, madonna, as if thy eldest
    son should be a fool, whose skull Jove cram with ~~Jupiter~~
    brains! For,—here he comes,—one of thy kin has a   110
    most weak pia mater. *brain*
    [*Enter Sir Toby.*]
Olivia: By mine honour, half drunk. What is he at the gate,
    cousin?
Sir Toby: A gentleman.
Olivia: A gentleman! What gentleman?   *a curse on* 115
Sir Toby: 'Tis a gentleman here—a plague o' these pickle-
    herring! How now, sot! *fool*
Feste: Good Sir Toby!
Olivia: Cousin, cousin, how have you come so early by this
    lethargy? *laziness / Drowsiness.*   120
Sir Toby: Lechery? I defy lechery. There's one at the gate.
Olivia: Ay, marry, what is he?
Sir Toby: Let him be the devil, an he will, I care not. Give
    me faith, say I. Well, it's all one.   [*Exit.*]
Olivia: What's a drunken man like, fool?   125
Feste: Like a drowned man, a fool, and a madman: one
    draught above heat makes him a fool; the second mads
    him; and a third drowns him.
Olivia: Go thou and seek the crowner, and let him sit o'
    my coz; for he's in the third degree of drink, he's   130
    drowned. Go, look after him.
Feste: He is but mad yet, madonna; and the fool shall look
    to the madman.   [*Exit.*]
    [*Re-enter Malvolio.*]
Malvolio: Madam, yond young fellow swears he will speak
    with you. I told him you were sick; he takes on him   135
    to understand so much, and therefore comes to speak
    with you. I told him you were asleep; he seems to
    have a foreknowledge of that too, and therefore comes
    to speak with you. What is to be said to him, lady?
    He's fortified against any denial.   140
Olivia: Tell him he shall not speak with me.
Malvolio: Has been told so; and he says, he'll stand at your
    door like a sheriff's post, and be the supporter to a
    bench, but he'll speak with you.

146   *of mankind:* an ordinary human being

147   *manner:* kind. Malvolio's answer puns on manners.

148-149 *will you/or no:* whether you want to or not

152   *squash:* unripe peascod (pea pod)

153   *codling:* unripe apple

153-154 *in/standing water:* at the turn of the tide, between ebb and flow, when no water is flowing in either direction

154-155 *well/favoured:* handsome, attractive; *shrewishly:* sharply

160   *embassy:* ambassador

165   *I would . . . away:* I do not want to waste

166   *for besides that:* for beside the fact that; *penned:* written

167   *con:* memorize

167-168 *let/me sustain no scorn:* do not abuse me

168   *comptible:* sensitive

169   *least sinister usage:* slightest mistreatment

171   *studied:* prepared (as an actor studies or prepares for a part)

173   *modest:* reasonable

175   *comedian:* actor

176   *my profound heart:* my wise lady

176-177 *by the very fangs/of malice:* Viola swears by all that is cruel (all the wicked accusations that could be made against her).

179   *I do not usurp myself:* I am not an imposter.

180   *you do usurp yourself:* You do betray yourself (by withholding yourself from Orsino).

181   *what:* your hand in marriage

Olivia: What kind o' man is he? 145
Malvolio: Why, of mankind. Ordinary human.
Olivia: What manner of man? kind
Malvolio: Of very ill manner; he'll speak with you, will you
    or no.
Olivia: Of what personage and years is he? 150
Malvolio: Not yet old enough for a man, nor young enough
    for a boy; as a squash is before 'tis a peascod, or a
    codling when 'tis almost an apple. 'Tis with him in
    standing water, between boy and man. He is very well
    favoured and he speaks very shrewishly; one would 155
    think his mother's milk were scarce out of him.

unripe apple

Olivia: Let him approach. Call in my gentlewoman.
Malvolio: Gentlewoman, my lady calls.   [*Exit.*]
    [*Re-enter Maria.*]
Olivia: Give me my veil. Come, throw it o'er my face. We'll
    once more hear Orsino's embassy. 160
    [*Enter Viola and Attendants.*]
Viola: The honourable lady of the house, which is she?
Olivia: Speak to me; I shall answer for her. Your will?
Viola: Most radiant, exquisite and unmatchable beauty,—I
    pray you, tell me if this be the lady of the house, for
    I never saw her. I would be loath to cast away my 165
    speech, for besides that it is excellently well penned, I
    have taken great pains to con it. Good beauties, let
    me sustain no scorn; I am very comptible, even to the
    least sinister usage.

Sensitive
Slightest
Mistreatment

Olivia: Whence came you, sir? 170
Viola: I can say little more than I have studied, and that
    question's out of my part. Good gentle one, give me
    modest assurance if you be the lady of the house, that
    I may proceed in my speech.
Olivia: Are you a comedian? *My wise lady.* 175
Viola: No, my profound heart; and yet, by the very fangs
    of malice I swear, I am not that I play. Are you the
    lady of the house?
Olivia: If I do not usurp myself, I am.
Viola: Most certain, if you are she, you do usurp yourself; 180
    for what is yours to bestow is not yours to reserve.

182	*this is from my commission:* I am not sticking to my instructions; *I will on:* I will continue
188	*like:* likely; *feigned:* dishonest, false
189-190	*allowed/your approach:* gave permission for you to enter
191	*reason:* sanity
192-193	*'Tis not . . . dialogue:* I am not in the mood to put up with trivial conversation.
194	*hoist sail:* prepare to depart (by putting up the sails)
195	*swabber:* sailor (who washes the deck); *hull:* remain (in harbour with sails furled)
196	*Some mollification for:* please pacify; *giant:* a sarcastic reference to the tiny Maria, who, like the giants in medieval folktales, is guarding her lady
199	*matter:* information
199-200	*when/the courtesy . . . fearful:* when your formality is so terrifying
200	*office:* business
201	*overture:* declaration
202	*taxation of homage:* demand for payment to a superior
207	*entertainment:* reception (by Sir Toby at the door)
208	*would:* want; *maidenhead:* virginity
209	*divinity:* a sacred message; *profanation:* a betrayal of Orsino's feelings (which should not be *profaned* or cheapened by revealing them to anyone but Olivia)
212	*text:* passage from the Bible that a preacher uses as the starting point for a sermon or message to the congregation
214	*comfortable doctrine:* comforting belief
216	*bosom:* heart
218	*by the method:* according to the custom (by citing the chapter and verse where the text may be found in the Bible)
219	*heresy:* false doctrine

Not sticking to instructions.

But this is from my commission. I will on with my
speech in your praise, and then show you the heart
of my message.

Olivia: Come to what is important in't; I forgive you the   185
    praise.

false / dishonest

Viola: Alas, I took great pains to study it, and 'tis poetical.

Olivia: It is the more like to be feigned; I pray you, keep
    it in. I heard you were saucy at my gates, and allowed
    your approach rather to wonder at you than to hear   190
    you. If you be not mad, be gone; if you have reason,
    be brief. 'Tis not that time of moon with me to make
    one in so skipping a dialogue.

sailor

Maria: Will you hoist sail, sir? Here lies your way.

Viola: No, good swabber; I am to hull here a little longer.   195
    Some mollification for your giant, sweet lady.

Olivia: Tell me your mind.   *Please pacify.*

Viola: I am a messenger.

Olivia: Sure, you have some hideous matter to deliver, when
    the courtesy of it is so fearful. Speak your office.   200

Viola: It alone concerns your ear. I bring no overture of

Demand payment

war, no taxation of homage. I hold the olive in my
    hand; my words are as full of peace as matter.

Olivia: Yet you began rudely. What are you? What would
    you?   205

Viola: The rudeness that hath appeared in me have I learned
    from my entertainment. What I am, and what I
    would, are as secret as maidenhead; to your ears,
    divinity; to any other's, profanation.

Olivia: Give us the place alone; we will hear this   210
    divinity,   [*Exeunt Maria and Attendants.*]
    Now, sir, what is your text?   *a sacred message.*

Viola: Most sweet lady,—

Olivia: A comfortable doctrine, and much may be said of
    it. Where lies your text?   215

Viola: In Orsino's bosom.

Olivia: In his bosom! In what chapter of his bosom?   *What chapter*

Viola: To answer by the method, in the first of his heart.   *of his heart*

Olivia: Oh, I have read it; it is heresy. Have you no more
    to say?   *Metaphor*   220

223   *out of your text:* off topic

224   *curtain:* See the note for Act 1, Scene 3, lines 116-117.

225   *this present:* just now

227   *if God did all:* if it is natural (without make-up)

228   *in grain:* ingrained, natural, permanent

229   *blent:* blended

230   *cunning:* skilful

232   *lead:* take

233   *copy:* duplicate (a child of similar beauty and grace)

235   *divers schedules:* various lists of articles for sale

236-237 *every particle . . . will:* Every item will be listed as an addition to my will.

237   *indifferent red:* fairly red

239   *praise:* appraise, evaluate

241   *if:* even if; *fair:* beautiful

243   *Could be but recompensed, though:* could never be fully rewarded, even though

244   *nonpareil:* unequalled (goddess or queen)

245   *fertile:* abundant

248   *I suppose him:* I consider him to be

250   *In voices well divulged:* well spoken of; *free:* generous

251   *in dimension . . . nature:* physically

252   *gracious:* graceful

254   *flame:* spirit

255   *deadly life:* a life like death

Viola: Good madam, let me see your face.

Olivia: Have you any commission from your lord to negotiate
with my face? You are now out of your text; but we
will draw the curtain and show you the picture. Look
you, sir, such a one I was this present. Is't not well   225
done?   [*Unveiling.*]

Viola: Excellently done, if God did all.

Olivia: 'Tis in grain, sir; 'twill endure wind and weather.

Viola: 'Tis beauty truly blent, whose red and white
Nature's own sweet and cunning hand laid on.   230
Lady, you are the cruell'st she alive,
If you will lead these graces to the grave
And leave the world no copy.

Olivia: Oh, sir, I will not be so hard-hearted; I will give
out divers schedules of my beauty. It shall be inven-   235
toried, and every particle and utensil labelled to my
will: as, item, two lips, indifferent red; item, two grey
eyes, with lids to them; item, one neck, one chin, and
so forth. Were you sent hither to praise me?

Viola: I see you what you are, you are too proud;   240
But, if you were the devil, you are fair.
My lord and master loves you. O, such love
Could be but recompensed, though you were crown'd
The nonpareil of beauty!

Olivia: How does he love me?

Viola: With adorations, fertile tears,   245
With groans that thunder love, with sighs of fire.

Olivia: Your lord does know my mind. I cannot love him;
Yet I suppose him virtuous, know him noble,
Of great estate, of fresh and stainless youth;
In voices well divulged, free, learn'd and valiant;   250
And in dimension and the shape of nature
A gracious person: but yet I cannot love him;
He might have took his answer long ago.

Viola: If I did love you in my master's flame,
With such a suffering, such a deadly life,   255
In your denial I would find no sense;
I would not understand it.

Olivia: Why, what would you?

258   *willow:* The willow tree is traditionally associated with the grief and heartbreak of unrequited love.

259   *my soul:* Olivia (who controls his very being)

260   *cantons:* songs (French *chansons*); *contemned:* rejected

262   *Halloo:* shout; *reverberate:* echoing

263   *babbling gossip of the air:* the echo (compared to an old gossip)

264-266 *you should . . . pity me:* You would not rest . . . unless you pitied me.

268   *state:* social rank

271   *perchance:* perhaps

274   *fee'd post:* messenger who accepts tips for his services

275   *recompense:* payment

276   *Love make . . . love:* I hope that Cupid (*Love*) makes the heart of the man you love as hard as flint.

277   *fervour:* strong love

283   *five-fold blazon:* a coat of arms consisting of five emblems; *soft:* slow down. (Olivia realizes how quickly she has fallen for the young Cesario.)

284   *Unless the . . . man:* if only Orsino were this man (I could love him)

290   *peevish:* impertinent

291   *county's:* Count's. Shakespeare refers to Orsino as Count more often than Duke.

292   *Would I or not:* whether I wanted it or not; *I'll none of it:* I don't want it.

Viola: Make me a willow cabin at your gate,
　And call upon my soul within the house;
　Write loyal cantons of contemned love　　　　　　260
　And sing them loud even in the dead of night;
　Halloo your name to the reverberate hills,
　And make the babbling gossip of the air
　Cry out "Olivia!" Oh, you should not rest
　Between the elements of air and earth,　　　　　　265
　But you should pity me!
Olivia:　　　　　　　　You might do much.
　What is your parentage?
Viola: Above my fortunes, yet my state is well;
　I am a gentleman.
Olivia:　　　　　　　Get you to your lord;
　I cannot love him. Let him send no more;
　Unless, perchance, you come to me again,　　　　270
　To tell me how he takes it. Fare you well.
　I thank you for your pains; spend this for me.
Viola: I am no fee'd post, lady; keep your purse.
　My master, not myself, lacks recompense.　　　　275
　Love make his heart of flint that you shall love;
　And let your fervour, like my master's, be
　Placed in contempt! Farewell, fair cruelty.　　　[*Exit.*]
Olivia: "What is your parentage?"
　"Above my fortunes, yet my state is well;　　　　280
　I am a gentleman." I'll be sworn thou art.
　Thy tongue, thy face, thy limbs, actions, and spirit,
　Do give thee five-fold blazon. Not too fast: soft, soft!
　Unless the master were the man. How now!
　Even so quickly may one catch the plague?　　　　285
　Methinks I feel this youth's perfections
　With an invisible and subtle stealth
　To creep in at mine eyes. Well, let it be.
　What ho, Malvolio!
　[*Re-enter Malvolio.*]
Malvolio:　　　　　　Here, madam, at your service.
Olivia: Run after that same peevish messenger,　　290
　The county's man. He left this ring behind him,
　Would I or not. Tell him I'll none of it.

293   *flatter with:* encourage

296   *Hie thee:* hurry

298-299 *fear to find/ . . . mind:* I am afraid that my eyes (through which
        love was believed to enter the soul) have betrayed my
        reason and good judgement.

300   *owe:* own. We are not in control of ourselves.

encourage

Desire him not to flatter with his lord,
Nor hold him up with hopes; I am not for him.
If that the youth will come this way to-morrow,   295
I'll give him reasons for't. Hie thee, Malvolio.
Malvolio: Madam, I will.   *hurry*   [*Exit.*]
Olivia: I do I know not what, and fear to find
Mine eye too great a flatterer for my mind.
Fate, show thy force; ourselves we do not owe.   300
What is decreed must be, and be this so.   [*Exit.*]

Rhyming Couplet

Rhyming Caplet.

Act 1, Scene 5: Activities

1. Though called a fool, Feste is really a professional comedian whose humour is based upon his keen perception of the foolishness of others. Why does he consider
   Olivia a fool? Why does Olivia defend him in his
   argument with Malvolio?

   a) Feste's kind of humour, called *satire*, is used today
      by many comedians. With a partner or in a small
      group, consider two or three with whom you are famil-
      iar. What kinds of behaviour and ways of thinking
      are the targets of their criticism?

   b) Write a short satirical piece of your own. Consider
      the following as possible targets: unnecessary
      school or community rules, overly harsh adult punish-
      ments, narrow-minded politicians, or boorish
      teenage behaviour.

2. a) Sir Toby is the dramatic stereotype of the "drunk."
      In groups of three or four, dramatize the scene in
      lines 114 to 133. How would you make Sir Toby
      funny?

   b) In a paragraph, compare Feste's humour in the first
      part of the scene with the humour of the part you
      have just dramatized. What do we laugh at in each
      case?

3. Ignoring the fact that Cesario is really a woman in
   disguise, what characteristics cause Olivia to fall so
   quickly in love with him?

   As Olivia, compose a letter to your dearest friend, confessing your feelings for the young Cesario, whom you have
   just met.

Be sure to add the characteristics of Cesario to the list of Viola's personality traits which you began in Activity 2, Scene 2 (page 20).

4. In Renaissance literature, women were described as goddesses to be worshipped and adored by men. Consider the imagery which Cesario uses in his praise and courtship of Olivia throughout this scene.

With this imagery in mind, complete the speech which Cesario begins in line 163 but does not finish: "Most radiant, exquisite and unmatchable beauty . . ." You may wish to include a short love poem as a part of your presentation to Olivia.

Act 1: Consider the Whole Act

1. Conflict, both external and internal, is the essence of drama. List all the conflicts which have arisen in Act 1. Compare your list with that of a partner and predict at least one resolution or outcome for each conflict.

2. In our daily lives, we often find ourselves playing roles determined by our own self-images or by the expectations of others. For example, teenagers often find themselves playing the "rebel" at home or at school. Similarly, in *Twelfth Night*, Olivia plays the role of the bereaved sister.

   a) With a partner, role-play two or three of the following situations to illustrate how people adjust their behaviour to fit the roles demanded of them:
      • A student requests an extension for an assignment from a teacher.
      • The same student justifies to a parent the reason for breaking a curfew.

- The same student responds to a friend who wants to cheat on a classroom test.
- The same student issues an athletic challenge to a student from a rival school.

b) Join pairs into groups of four and discuss the following questions:
- How do the situations determine the roles we play?
- How important are the expectations of others in determining our roles?
- How important are our own values in determining the roles we play?
- What happens when our true values are in conflict with the role we are expected to play?

c) Consider one or two of these characters: Olivia, Orsino, Sir Andrew, Feste.
- What role does the character play?
- What values does the character seem to have?
- What values, then, does the character consider insignificant?
Give examples from the play to support your answers.

d) Summarize your discussion and present your conclusions to the rest of the class. In your journal, make an entry entitled "The Roles People Play."

3. Although some scholars have suggested a geographical location for it, you won't find the land of Illyria on any map of the world. Based on your reading of the first act, what is "fantastical" or unreal about Illyria? What aspects of Illyria remind you of the real world? As a citizen of Illyria, record your diary entry for a typical day in this strange but familiar land.

4. ". . . yet, a beaful strife!
Whoe'er I woo, myself would be his wife."
(Scene 4, lines 41–42)

Because of her disguise as Cesario, Viola cannot act upon her feelings and finds herself in a seemingly impossible situation.

As Viola, compose a journal entry in which you outline your situation and consider the options open to you. Be sure to weigh the consequences both of remaining in disguise and of revealing your true identity.

5. Select a scene or part of a scene from Act 1 which appeals to you. As a director, prepare the scene for presentation. Be sure to consider the following questions:
   - Why have you chosen this scene? What are the main ideas and feelings which you wish to convey to your audience?
   - How will you communicate these ideas and feelings? What type of presentation will you choose (modern English version, Shakespearean form, soap opera, pantomime)?
   - Who will you choose to play the various parts? How will you help them to show the relationships among the characters?

   Working with a small group, prepare and rehearse your scene for presentation to the class.

For the next scene . . .

"A friend in need is a friend indeed!"
What is the meaning of this famous proverb? How has your experience or that of someone you know proven it true?

Act 2, Scene 1

In this scene . . .

Sebastian, twin brother of Viola, has survived the shipwreck which he believes has taken the life of his
sister. With Antonio, another kind and generous sea
captain, he has landed safely on the sea coast of
Illyria. He tells Antonio about himself and his sadness
over his sister's death. Antonio decides to accompany Sebastian to the court of Count Orsino, in spite
of great danger to his own life.

1-2	*Nor will . . . you?:* Don't you wish me to go with you?
3	*By your patience:* with your permission
3-4	*My stars . . . me:* I am unlucky.
4	*malignancy:* disease or evil; here, bad luck
5	*distemper:* infect, disorder; *crave:* desire
6	*leave:* permission
7	*recompense:* repayment
8	*whither:* where
9	*sooth:* truly; *determinate voyage:* the course of action that I have planned and am determined to follow
10	*extravagancy:* aimless wandering
10-11	*so excellent a touch/of modesty:* such good manners
11-12	*what I/ . . . keep in:* my secrets (what I would like to keep to myself)
12-13	*it charges . . . myself:* Common courtesy requires that I should disclose my identity and background.
17	*in an hour:* within an hour (he and Viola are twins)
19	*some hour:* about an hour
20	*breach:* breakers, waves
24	*estimable wonder:* admiring judgement; *overfar:* too far, too much
25	*publish:* describe
28	*with more:* salt water (in the form of salt tears)
29	*Pardon me . . . entertainment:* Please, forgive me for the poor hospitality you have received from me.
30	*forgive me your trouble:* Please, forgive me the trouble I have caused you.

Act 2, Scene 1

The sea-coast.

Enter Antonio and Sebastian.

Antonio: Will you stay no longer? Nor will you not that I
go with you?

Sebastian: By your patience, no. My stars shine darkly
over me. The malignancy of my fate might perhaps
distemper yours; therefore I shall crave of you your   5
leave that I may bear my evils alone. It were a bad
recompense for your love, to lay any of them on you.

Antonio: Let me know of you whither you are bound.

Sebastian: No, sooth, sir. My determinate voyage is mere
extravagancy. But I perceive in you so excellent a touch   10
of modesty, that you will not extort from me what I
am willing to keep in; therefore it charges me in manners the rather to express myself. You must know of
me then, Antonio, my name is Sebastian, which I called
Roderigo. My father was that Sebastian of Messaline,   15
whom I know you have heard of. He left behind him
myself and a sister, both born in an hour. If the heavens had been pleased, would we had so ended! But you,
sir, altered that; for some hour before you took me
from the breach of the sea was my sister drowned.   20

Antonio: Alas the day!

Sebastian: A lady, sir, though it was said she much resembled
me, was yet of many accounted beautiful; but, though
I could not with such estimable wonder overfar believe that, yet thus far I will boldly publish her; she   25
bore a mind that envy could not but call fair. She is
drowned already, sir, with salt water, though I seem
to drown her remembrance again with more.

Antonio: Pardon me, sir, your bad entertainment.

Sebastian: O good Antonio, forgive me your trouble.   30

31-32   *If you . . . servant:* If you do not want to be the cause of my death (by forcing our separation), let me serve you. (Antonio wishes to help his new friend; he does not seek employment in the literal sense.)

34   *recovered:* rescued, saved

35   *kindness:* tender emotion

36   *yet:* still; *the manners of my mother:* the behaviour of a woman

37-38   *will tell tales/of me:* will reveal how I feel (that is, I will burst into tears of sorrow)

38   *bound to:* headed for

Antonio: If you will not murder me for my love, let me be
    your servant.

Sebastian: If you will not undo what you have done, that
    is, kill him whom you have recovered, desire it not.
    Fare ye well at once: my bosom is full of kindness,   35
    and I am yet so near the manners of my mother, that
    upon the least occasion more mine eyes will tell tales
    of me. I am bound to the Count Orsino's court.
    Farewell.   [*Exit.*]

Antonio: The gentleness of all the gods go with thee!   40
    I have many enemies in Orsino's court,
    Else would I very shortly see thee there.
    But, come what may, I do adore thee so,
    That danger shall seem sport, and I will go.   [*Exit.*]

Act 2, Scene 1: Activities

1. Antonio bears an obvious resemblance to Viola's sea captain in Act 1, Scene 2. In Shakespeare's plays, sea captains display a common set of stereotypical personality and character traits. Based on the two figures you have met in this play, what are the features of this stage stereotype?

   With a partner, consider how the public perception of real sea captains might have led to this stereotype. Compare your ideas with those of another pair.

   Make a list of positive stereotypes in our contemporary world. How accurately do you think these stereotypes reflect the real lives of these men and women?

2. In Shakespeare's plays, shorter scenes are often used to provide background information and to prepare the audience for later plot developments.

   With a partner or in a small group, review this scene and list all the pieces of information this scene provides, both directly (in the dialogue) and indirectly (through the behaviour of the characters).

   Select those details that you think will be significant to further developments of the plot. Predict how the plot might be affected by these details.

For the next scene . . .

What exactly is a *dilemma?* What (if any) dilemma have you found yourself in recently? How did you resolve your difficulty?

Act 2, Scene 2

In this scene . . .

As instructed by Olivia, Malvolio catches up to Cesario/
Viola in the street in order to "return" Olivia's ring to
Cesario. Viola resists taking the ring and is puzzled
by Olivia's deception. She then realizes that Olivia
has fallen in love with her.

2   *on a moderate pace:* walking with reasonable speed

3   *but hither:* just here, only this far

7   *desperate assurance;* hopeless certainty; *she will none of him:* she will have nothing to do with him

8   *hardy:* bold

10   *this:* Olivia's message to Orsino; *it:* the ring

11   *of me:* from me. (Why does Viola react so quickly to protect Olivia?)

14   *in your eye:* in plain sight (on the ground)

17   *outside:* outward appearance (as Cesario)

18   *made good view of me:* took a good look at me

19   *lost:* caused her to lose

20   *in starts:* in incomplete thoughts

21   *cunning:* craftiness

22   *Invites:* tries to attract; *in:* by means of; *churlish:* surly, ill-bred

27   *pregnant enemy:* Satan, who is " pregnant" with (or full of) wicked plans and tricks

28   *proper-false:* suitors who are handsome but deceitful

29   *waxen:* impressionable; *to set their forms:* to make an impression

Scene 2

A street.

Enter Viola, Malvolio following.

Malvolio: Were not you even now with the Countess Olivia?

Viola: Even now, sir; on a moderate pace I have since
arrived but hither. ~~This far~~ [*handwritten:* This far]

Malvolio: She returns this ring to you, sir. You might have
saved me my pains, to have taken it away yourself. 5
She adds, moreover, that you should put your lord into
a desperate assurance she will none of him; and one
thing more, that you be never so hardy to come again
in his affairs, unless it be to report your lord's taking
of this. Receive it so. [*handwritten:* Carelessly threw it to her.] 10

Viola: She took the ring of me; I'll none of it.

Malvolio: Come, sir, you peevishly threw it to her; and her
will is, it should be so returned. If it be worth stoop- [*handwritten:* looking for]
ing for, there it lies in your eye; if not, be it his that
finds it. [*handwritten:* returned in same manner.] [*Exit.*] 15

Viola: I left no ring with her. What means this lady?
Fortune forbid my outside have not charm'd her!
She made good view of me; indeed, so much
That sure methought her eyes had lost her tongue,
For she did speak in starts distractedly. 20
She loves me, sure; the cunning of her passion
Invites me in this churlish messenger. [*handwritten:* Surly ill bred]
None of my lord's ring! Why, he sent her none.
I am the man! If it be so, as 'tis,
Poor lady, she were better love a dream. 25
Disguise, I see, thou art a wickedness, [*handwritten:* Satan full of bad ideas!]
Wherein the pregnant enemy does much.
How easy is it for the proper-false [*handwritten:* handsome yet]
In women's waxen hearts to set their forms! [*handwritten:* deceitful people]
Alas, our frailty is the cause, not we! [*handwritten:* can suck women]
For such as we are made of, such we be. 30 [*handwritten:* in to their trapps]

[*handwritten margin notes:* Finishing off act scenes / he thinks that she's in love with him. / Gave him it. / Blank Verse.]

[*handwritten bottom note:* With, a disguise Cesario can do wicked things.]

32   *fadge:* turn out

33   *monster:* Viola calls herself this because she is both man and woman at the same time; *fond:* dote

36   *my state is desperate for:* I have no hope of winning

38   *thriftless:* wasted

Blank verse: Iambic pentameter lines which are not regularly rhyming.

Turn out

Man + Woman

How will this fadge? My master loves her dearly;
And I, poor monster, fond as much on him;
And she, mistaken, seems to dote on me.
What will become of this? As I am man, 35
My state is desperate for my master's love;
As I am woman,—now alas the day!—
What thriftless sighs shall poor Olivia breathe!
O Time, thou must untangle this, not I!
It is too hard a knot for me to untie! [*Exit.*] 40

fond

No I have hope of winning

Wasted

Soliloquy : is a speech which is directed to the audience by a character alone on the stage; it gives the character's thoughts (cf, aside)

Act 2, Scene 2: Activities

1. A *soliloquy* is a speech in which a character thinks aloud while alone on stage. It is intended to reveal the thoughts and feelings of the speaker to the audience. Reread Viola's soliloquy in this scene (lines 16–40). What does it reveal about her thoughts and feelings?

   Rewrite the speech as you think a modern Viola would say it. Present a dramatic reading of your new soliloquy to a small group. Compare your version with those of others in the group and discuss the different interpretations.

2. a) In a journal entry, outline how *you* would "untie the knot" or resolve the dilemma if you were Viola.

   b) In a separate entry, predict what you think *Viola* will do in the play.

3. Love triangles are a common device in fiction and drama. In a small group, brainstorm examples of love triangles in books, movies, or television. In what ways is the situation with Orsino, Olivia, and Viola/Cesario like a typical love triangle? In what ways is it unusual?

   In groups of two or three, create a plot which hinges on a love triangle. Find an appropriate format for the telling of your story: tabloid newspaper article, soap opera, talk show, romantic fiction, ballad, or revue sketch.

For the next scene . . .

When someone in authority orders you to stop having fun, what is your reaction? How might the reactions of characters in television and movie comedies be different from your own? Are characters in literature confined by the same rules and expectations as we are? Discuss your ideas.

Act 2, Scene 3

In this scene . . .

Sir Toby and Sir Andrew continue to spend their nights in drunken revelry. Feste joins them and sings a song about the pleasures of young love. Maria comes to warn them that Olivia is increasingly displeased with their behaviour, but they ignore her good advice. Finally Malvolio appears in his capacity as steward or manager of Olivia's household and gives them a formal warning. He also threatens to report Maria to Olivia, for her assumed participation. Maria reveals a plan to make a fool of Malvolio by playing upon his arrogance and ambition. She is also aware of Malvolio's attraction for Olivia. She will compose a love letter in the handwriting of Olivia and arrange for Malvolio to find it. Malvolio's discovery of Olivia's love, Maria promises, will provide the perfect opportunity for revenge.

1 *a-bed:* in bed

2 *betimes:* early; *"diluculo surgere":* Toby quotes a portion of a Latin proverb – it is very healthy to rise early.

4 *by my troth:* to speak truly

6 *false:* faulty, illogical; *can:* tankard, mug

9 *the four elements?:* earth, air, fire, and water, which were thought to be the basic ingredients of all things

10 *Faith:* it's true

13 *stoup:* flagon, beaker

15-16 *the picture/of "We three"?:* a common illustration for an inn's sign. It featured two fools or asses and was inscribed 'we three.' The viewer was the third. Feste is suggesting that he, Sir Toby, and Sir Andrew are asses.

17 *catch:* song

18 *breast:* voice

22-23 *Pigrogromitus . . . Vapians . . . Queubus:* These characters and places appear to have been invented by Feste as part of last night's "gracious fooling."

24 *leman:* sweetheart

25 *I did empeticos thy gratillity:* more of the clown's fooling, meaning something like, "I pocketed your tip." The following statements, however, are pure nonsense.

26 *whipstock:* handle of whip

27 *Myrmidons:* followers of the Greek hero Achilles

Scene 3

Olivia's house.

Enter Sir Toby and Sir Andrew.

[handwritten: Joking around, in bed]

Sir Toby: Approach, Sir Andrew. Not to be a-bed after
midnight is to be up betimes; and "diluculo surgere",
thou know'st,— *[handwritten: Healthy to rise early]*

Sir Andrew: Nay, by my troth, I know not; but I know, to
be up late is to be up late. 5

Sir Toby: A false conclusion. I hate it as an unfilled can.
To be up after midnight and to go to bed then, is early;
so that to go to bed after midnight is to go to bed *[handwritten: It's just]*
betimes. Does not our life consist of the four elements? *[handwritten: Earth, air, fire, water]*

Sir Andrew: Faith, so they say; but I think it rather con-
sists of eating and drinking. *[handwritten: life's elements are eating, sleeping, drinking]* 10

Sir Toby: Thou'rt a scholar; let us therefore eat and drink.
Marian, I say! a stoup of wine!

[*Enter Feste.*]

Sir Andrew: Here comes the fool, i' faith.

Feste: How now, my hearts! did you never see the picture 15
of "We three"? *[handwritten: If you call me a fool, what are you?]*

Sir Toby: Welcome, ass. Now let's have a catch.

Sir Andrew: By my troth, the fool has an excellent breast. *[handwritten: Nice voice]*
I had rather than forty shillings I had such a leg, and
so sweet a breath to sing, as the fool has. In sooth, 20
thou wast in very gracious fooling last night, when thou
spokest of Pigrogromitus, of the Vapians passing the *[handwritten: invented by Feste]*
equinoctial of Queubus. 'Twas very good, i' faith. I sent
thee sixpence for thy leman. Hadst it? *[handwritten: Sweetheart]*

Feste: I did impeticos thy gratillity: for Malvolio's nose is *[handwritten: I pocketed your tip]* 25
no whipstock; my lady has a white hand, and the *[handwritten: Handle of no whip]*
Myrmidons are no bottle-ale houses. *[handwritten: None-sense]*

Sir Andrew: Excellent! why, this is the best fooling, when
all is done. Now, a song.

[handwritten: Followers of the Greek hero Achilles]

32	*testril:* tester, a coin worth sixpence
34	*song of good life:* Feste suggests a song about life's pleasures. Sir Andrew, however, thinks that Feste is suggesting a song about virtuous living or the moral life.
40	*Trip:* skip; *sweeting:* sweet one
42	*Every wise man's son:* every fool. The popular belief was that wise men had fools for sons.
45	*'Tis not hereafter:* It is not something to be put off for the future.
47	*still:* always
48	*plenty:* profit, advantage
49	*sweet and twenty:* sweet and twenty times sweet
51	*mellifluous:* smooth as honey
52	*contagious breath:* catchy tune
54	*To hear . . . contagion:* If we were to listen with our noses, the clown's " breath" would smell sweet (not foul, as diseased or *contagious* breaths usually are).
55	*welkin:* skies
56-57	*draw three/souls:* Fine music was believed to draw the soul out of the body.
57	*weaver:* Weavers were noted for their singing, particularly of hymns and psalms.
58	*An:* if; *dog:* clever. In the following line, Feste takes the word literally as " latches, or catching devices."
62	*constrained:* forced
64-65	*Hold thy/peace:* Be silent.

Sir Toby: Come on; there is sixpence for you—let's have a   30
    song.

    tester [handwritten]

Sir Andrew: There's a testril of me too. If one knight give
    a—
Feste: Would you have a love song, or a song of good life?
Sir Toby: A love song, a love song.   35
Sir Andrew: Ay, ay. I care not for good life.
Feste: *O mistress mine, where are you roaming?*
        O, stay and hear; your true love's coming,
            That can sing both high and low.
        Trip no further, pretty sweeting;   40
        Journeys end in lovers meeting,
        Every wise man's son doth know.

Sir Andrew: Excellent good, i' faith.
Sir Toby: Good, good.
Feste: *What is love? 'Tis not hereafter;*   45
        Present mirth hath present laughter;
            What's to come is still unsure.
        In delay there lies no plenty;
        Then come kiss me, sweet and twenty,
            Youth's a stuff will not endure.   50

    flows like honey [handwritten]

Sir Andrew: A mellifluous voice, as I am true knight.
Sir Toby: A contagious breath.   *catchy voice   soft + sweet* [handwritten]
Sir Andrew: Very sweet and contagious, i' faith.
Sir Toby: To hear by the nose, it is dulcet in contagion.   *skies* [handwritten]
    But shall we make the welkin dance indeed? Shall we   55
    rouse the night-owl in a catch that will draw three
    souls out of one weaver? Shall we do that?
Sir Andrew: An you love me, let's do't. I am dog at a catch.
Feste: By'r lady, sir, and some dogs will catch well.
Sir Andrew: Most certain. Let our catch be, "Thou knave".   60
Feste: "Hold thy peace, thou knave," knight? I shall be
    constrained in't to call thee knave, knight.

    Round [handwritten]
    Hold thy peace thou knave [handwritten]

Sir Andrew: 'Tis not the first time I have constrained one
    to call me knave. Begin, fool. It begins *Hold thy
    peace.*
Feste: I shall never begin if I hold my peace.
Sir Andrew: Good, i' faith. Come, begin.

    Make up music [handwritten]

                            [*They join. They sing.*]

Pun [handwritten]

69   *caterwauling:* screaming (most often with regard to cats!)

70   *bid:* asked, ordered

72   *Cataian:* a person from Cathay or China, here used to mean a villain. (Toby's stereotype is probably based upon the image of a medieval Chinese war-lord); *politicians:* skilful and cunning

73   *Peg-a-Ramsey:* a comic character in a popular song of Shakespeare's day

74   *consanguineous:* of the same blood or family (as Olivia)

74   *Tillyvally:* nonsense, fiddle-faddle

76   *Beshrew me:* a mild oath

79   *natural:* naturally (with an unintentional pun on *natural*, a term for a fool or idiot)

83   *wit:* common sense; *honesty:* common decency

84   *tinkers:* tinsmiths

85   *coziers':* cobblers', shoemakers'

86   *mitigation or remorse:* lowering or softening. (Shakespeare seems to be using *remorse* in its literal Latin sense of "biting back.")

88   *Sneck up:* Go hang yourself!

89   *round:* blunt

90   *harbours you:* lets you stay

91   *she's nothing allied:* she is not a supporter of

92   *misdemeanours:* misdeeds (bad behaviour)

96-106 The italicized lines in this passage indicate that the lines are sung. Sir Toby and Feste offer spontaneous variations on a popular song of Shakespeare's day, "Corydon's Farewell to Phyllis."

[Handwritten: Don't trust me if Olv. comes to kick Mal. out.]

[Enter Maria.] *[Handwritten: Screaming]*

Maria: What a caterwauling do you keep here! If my lady
  have not called up her steward Malvolio and bid him 70
  turn you out of doors, never trust me— *[Handwritten: Villain]*

Sir Toby: My lady's a Cataian, we are politicians, Malvolio's
  a Peg-a-Ramsey, and *Three merry men be we.* Am not I
  consanguineous? Am I not of her blood? Tillyvally!
  Lady! *There dwelt a man in Babylon, lady, lady!* 75

[Handwritten right margin: Nonsense fiddle faddle / Comic character in popular songs]

Feste: Beshrew me, the knight's in admirable fooling.

Sir Andrew: Ay, he does well enough if he be disposed, and
  so do I too. He does it with a better grace, but I do it
  more natural.

Sir Toby: *Oh, the twelfth day of December,—* 80

Maria: For the love o' God, peace!

  [Enter Malvolio.]

Malvolio: My masters, are you mad? Or what are you? Have
  you no wit, manners, nor honesty, but to gabble like
  tinkers at this time of night? Do ye make an ale-house
  of my lady's house, that ye squeak out your coziers' 85
  catches without any mitigation or remorse of voice? Is
  there no respect of place, persons, nor time in you?

[Handwritten: Tinsmith] [Handwritten: Cobblers/Shoemaker] [Handwritten: Clock] [Handwritten: disrespectful]

Sir Toby: We did keep time, sir, in our catches. Sneck up!

[Handwritten: Hang yourself]

Malvolio: Sir Toby, I must be round with you. My lady
  bade me tell you, that, though she harbours you as her 90
  kinsman, she's nothing allied to your disorders. If you
  can separate yourself and your misdemeanours, you are
  welcome to the house; if not, an it would please you
  to take leave of her, she is very willing to bid you
  farewell. 95

[Handwritten: Put music beat] [Handwritten: noise / Here comes / get in the middle of it.] [Handwritten: Bad behavior]

Sir Toby: *Farewell, dear heart, since I must needs be gone.*

Maria: *Nay, good Sir Toby.*

Feste: *His eyes do show his days are almost done.*

Malvolio: *Is't even so?*

Sir Toby: *But I will never die.* 100

Feste: *Sir Toby, there you lie.*

Malvolio: This is much credit to you.

Sir Toby: *Shall I bid him go?*

Feste: *What an if you do?*

Sir Toby: *Shall I bid him go, and spare not?* 105

Feste: *Oh, no, no, no, no, you dare not!*

110   *ginger:* often used as a spice for ale. Ginger was also considered to be an aphrodisiac.

111   *Saint Anne:* mother of the Virgin Mary. This was a common oath of Shakespeare's day.

112-113 *rub your chain with/crumbs:* Go and polish your chain of office (remember that you are only a servant).

114   *prized:* valued

115-116 *give/means . . . rule:* support this brawling behaviour (by supplying the drink)

118   *Go shake your ears:* Maria's insult suggests that Malvolio is an ass.

120   *the field:* to a duel

126   *out of quiet:* upset

127   *gull:* trick; *nayword:* byword, proverb. Maria promises to make Malvolio's name synonymous with "fool."

128   *recreation:* source of amusement

131   *Possess:* tell, inform

132   *puritan:* a Protestant sect that flourished in England, despite almost constant persecution, during the late 16th and 17th centuries. The Puritans were strict moralists who disapproved of any thinking or behaviour that was not in keeping with their interpretation of the Bible. Today, the adjective *puritan* is used to describe persons who are extremely strict about their religious and moral beliefs.

139   *time-pleaser:* poser, pretender; *affectioned:* affected, artificial

139-140 *cons state/without book:* memorizes the ways of the court

140   *by great swarths:* in large chunks

140-141 *the best/persuaded of himself:* convinced of his own importance

142   *grounds of faith:* belief, conviction

143   *vice:* weakness

146   *obscure:* difficult to understand; *epistles:* letters

Sir Toby: Out o' tune, sir! Ye lie. Art any more than a
    steward? Dost thou think, because thou art virtuous,
    there shall be no more cakes and ale?

Feste: Yes, by St. Anne, and ginger shall be hot i' the mouth   110
    too.

Sir Toby: Thou'rt i' the right. Go, sir, rub your chain with
    crumbs. A stoup of wine, Maria!

Malvolio: Mistress Mary, if you prized my lady's favour at
    anything more than contempt, you would not give   115
    means for this uncivil rule. She shall know of it, by this
    hand.   [*Exit.*]

Maria: Go shake your ears.

Sir Andrew: 'Twere as good a deed as to drink when a man's
    a-hungry, to challenge him the field, and then to   120
    break promise with him and make a fool of him.

Sir Toby: Do't, knight. I'll write thee a challenge; or I'll
    deliver thy indignation to him by word of mouth.

Maria: Sweet Sir Toby, be patient for to-night. Since the
    youth of the count's was to-day with my lady, she is   125
    much out of quiet. For Monsieur Malvolio, let me
    alone with him; if I do not gull him into a nayword,
    and make him a common recreation, do not think I
    have wit enough to lie straight in my bed. I know I can
    do it.   130

Sir Toby: Possess us, possess us; tell us something of him.

Maria: Marry, sir, sometimes he is a kind of puritan.

Sir Andrew: Oh, if I thought that, I'd beat him like a dog!

Sir Toby: What, for being a puritan? Thy exquisite reason,
    dear knight.   135

Sir Andrew: I have no exquisite reason for't, but I have
    reason good enough.

Maria: The devil a puritan that he is, or anything constantly,
    but a time-pleaser, an affectioned ass, that cons state
    without book and utters it by great swarths: the best   140
    persuaded of himself, so crammed, as he thinks, with
    excellencies, that it is his grounds of faith that all that
    look on him love him; and on that vice in him will
    my revenge find notable cause to work.

Sir Toby: What wilt thou do?   145

Maria: I will drop in his way some obscure epistles of love,

148   *manner of his gait:* way he walks; *expressure:* expression

149-150 *most/feelingly personated:* very accurately depicted, described

151-152 *on a forgotten . . . hands:* If we find an old note we've forgotten about, we can't tell whose handwriting we're looking at.

153   *device:* trick

158   *a horse of that colour:* something like that. (Think of the expression "a horse of a different colour.")

162   *Sport royal:* entertainment fit for royalty; *I warrant you:* I promise you; *physic:* medicine

163   *plant:* hide

165   *construction:* interpretation

167   *Penthesilea:* queen of the Amazons, a tribe of tall warrior women. This is another joking reference to Maria's height.

168   *Before me:* I swear (with myself as witness)

169   *beagle:* small hound

174   *recover:* win

174-175 *a foul way/out:* in a real mess (specifically, a great deal poorer)

177   *cut:* a gelding (a castrated horse)

180   *burn:* heat (with spices); *sack:* a dry white wine

wherein, by the colour of his beard, the shape of his
leg, the manner of his gait, the expressure of his eye,
forehead, and complexion, he shall find himself most
feelingly personated. I can write very like my lady
your niece; on a forgotten matter we can hardly make   150
distinction of our hands.

Sir Toby: Excellent! I smell a device.

Sir Andrew: I have't in my nose too.

Sir Toby: He shall think, by the letters that thou wilt drop,   155
that they come from my niece, and that she's in love
with him.

Maria: My purpose is, indeed, a horse of that colour.

Sir Andrew: And your horse now would make him an ass.

Maria: Ass, I doubt not.   160

Sir Andrew: Oh, 'twill be admirable!

Maria: Sport royal, I warrant you. I know my physic will
work with him. I will plant you two, and let the fool
make a third, where he shall find the letter. Observe his
construction of it. For this night, to bed, and dream   165
on the event. Farewell.   [*Exit.*]

Sir Toby: Good night, Penthesilea.

Sir Andrew: Before me, she's a good wench.

Sir Toby: She's a beagle, true-bred, and one that adores
me. What o' that?   170

Sir Andrew: I was adored once too.

Sir Toby: Let's to bed, knight. Thou hadst need send for
more money.

Sir Andrew: If I cannot recover your niece, I am a foul way
out.   175

Sir Toby: Send for money, knight. If thou hast her not i'
the end, call me cut.

Sir Andrew: If I do not, never trust me, take it how you
will.

Sir Toby: Come, come, I'll go burn some sack; 'tis too late   180
to go to bed now. Come, knight; come, knight.

[*Exeunt.*]

91

Act 2, Scene 3: Activities

1. Sir Andrew compliments Feste on his vivid tale about "Pigrogromitus, of the Vapians passing the/equinoctial of Queubus" (lines 22–23). Using Feste's terminology as a starting point, compose the imaginary adventure that so impressed Andrew. Share your story with a partner.

2. a) What does Feste's song, "O Mistress Mine," have to say about life and love? How is it typical of love songs? Compile a list of similar lyrics from popular songs. Select one to play or read to your class. Comment on the thematic parallels between your selection and "O Mistress Mine."

   b) As an alternative, you might compose music for the song and present it to the class live or on tape.

3. Reread the confrontation between Malvolio and the revellers (lines 82–117). With whom do you sympathize and why? What is it about Malvolio that makes Maria and her friends want to plot revenge against him? Complete the following:
   - In groups of five, play this short scene several times, exploring the qualities in Malvolio's character which others find disagreeable.
   - How many ways can you play the role? How can you play the scene to make Malvolio a sympathetic character?
   - Decide which interpretation of the scene works best. In a director's log book, explain and defend your interpretation.

4. What is your impression of Maria's plan? Will it be good fun or cruel embarrassment? Would *you* go along with it? Why or why not? Record your responses in a journal entry. Be sure to consider Malvolio's point of view.

5. "I will drop in his way some obscure epistles of love . . ."
   (line 146)
   As Maria, write one of these love letters from Olivia to
   Malvolio. Remember that your aim is to "catch" him.

For the next scene . . .

During Shakespeare's lifetime, how were the attitudes of
men and women towards love different? How did their
behaviour in social situations reflect these differences
of viewpoint? Have the attitudes of men and women
changed? If so, in what ways? In what ways do men's
"traditional" attitudes towards love persist?

Act 2, Scene 4

In this scene . . .

Orsino continues to suffer the torments of unrequited love. Feste sings to him a tragic ballad about the loyalty of a faithful but rejected lover. Meanwhile, Orsino lectures Cesario/Viola about the nature of love, claiming that love affects men and women in very different ways. Viola comes close to confessing her love for Orsino, but her disguise as Cesario, of course, protects her from discovery. At the end of the scene, Cesario/Viola is sent to resume the courtship of Olivia on Orsino's behalf.

1   *morrow:* morning

2   *but:* only

3   *antique:* quaint

5   *light airs:* trivial melodies; *recollected terms:* studies and artificial musical compositions

18   *Unstaid:* unsteady; *skittish:* nervous, fidgety (usually used of horses); *all motions else:* all other emotions

19   *Save:* except; *image:* vision

21-22   *the seat/ . . . throned:* the heart. (See also Act 1, Scene 1, line 38.)

23   *My life upon't:* I would stake my life upon it.

24   *stay'd upon some favour:* rested on some face

Scene 4

Duke Orsino's palace.

*Enter Duke, Viola, Curio,
and others.*

coherence → wants love

Duke: Give me some music. Now, good-morrow, friends. *morning*
Now, good Cesario, but that piece of song,
That old and antique song we heard last night. *only*
Methought it did relieve my passion much,
More than light airs and recollected terms 5
Of these most brisk and giddy-paced times.
Come, but one verse.
Curio: He is not here, so please your lordship, that should
sing it. *Person who sings is not there.*
Duke: Who was it? 10
Curio: Feste, the jester, my lord; a fool that the lady
Olivia's father took much delight in. He is about
the house.
Duke: Seek him out, and play the tune the while.

[*Exit Curio. Music plays.*]

Come hither, boy. If ever thou shalt love, 15
In the sweet pangs of it remember me;
For such as I am all true lovers are,
Unstaid and skittish in all motions else,
Save in the constant image of the creature
That is beloved. How dost thou like this tune?
Viola: It gives a very echo to the seat
Where Love is throned.
Duke: I would stake my Thou dost speak masterly.
My life upon't, young though thou art, thine eye
Hath stay'd upon some favour that it loves.
Hath it not, boy? *rested on some face*

quaint
un-steady
Nervous
All other emotions
Startes talking about love
the heart (Act 1 scene 1, line 38).
DRAMATIC IRONY
She loves him but he doesn't know it
Trivial melodies studies artificial musical composition

25   *by your favour:* if you please (with "like your face" as a hidden meaning)

26   *Of your complexion:* like you. (*Complexion* is used throughout the play to mean "nature" or "personality.")

27   *What years, i' faith:* How old is she? tell me truly

29   *still:* always

30   *so wears she to him:* She adapts herself to him (and learns to love him).

31   *So sways . . . heart:* She remains steady in her husband's affections.

33   *fancies:* desires

34   *worn:* worn out, exhausted

37   *cannot hold the bent:* cannot stand the strain (as a weak bow cannot withstand the strain of being bent back)

39   *display'd:* opened (in full bloom)

41   *even when:* just as

44   *spinsters:* spinners

45   *free:* carefree; *bones:* implements, made from bone, used for making lace

46   *Do use to chant it:* often sing it; *silly sooth:* simple truth

48   *Like the old age:* as in the good old days

51   *Come away:* Come to me.

52   *cypress:* coffin made of cypress wood. (The cypress was associated with death.)

53   *Fly away:* Be gone.

55   *stuck all with yew:* covered with leaves of the yew tree. (The yew, like the cypress, was emblematic of death.)

Viola: A little, by your favour.

Duke: What kind of woman is't?

Viola: Of your complexion.

Duke: She is not worth thee, then. What years, i' faith?

Viola: About your years, my lord.

Duke: Too old, by heaven. Let still the woman take
    An elder than herself; so wears she to him,
    So sways she level in her husband's heart.
    For, boy, however we do praise ourselves,
    Our fancies are more giddy and unfirm,
    More longing, wavering, sooner lost and worn,
    Than women's are.

Viola: I think it well, my lord.

Duke: Then let thy love be younger than thyself
    Or thy affection cannot hold the bent;
    For women are as roses, whose fair flower
    Being once display'd, doth fall that very hour.

Viola: And so they are. Alas, that they are so;
    To die, even when they to perfection grow!

[Re-enter Curio and Feste.]

Duke: O fellow, come, the song we had last night.
    Mark it, Cesario, it is old and plain;
    The spinsters and the knitters in the sun,
    And the free maids that weave their thread with bones
    Do use to chant it. It is silly sooth,
    And dallies with the innocence of love,
    Like the old age.

Feste: Are you ready, sir?

Duke: Ay; prithee, sing.   [Music.] 50

Feste: *Come away, come away, death,*
       And in sad cypress let me be laid;
    Fly away, fly away, breath;
       I am slain by a fair cruel maid.
    My shroud of white, stuck all with yew,
          O prepare it!
    My part of death, no one so true
          Did share it.

    Not a flower, not a flower sweet,
       On my black coffin let there be strown;   60

99

67   *pains:* trouble

70   *pleasure will be paid:* Feste quotes part of the popular proverb, "Pleasure will be paid for with pain."

73   *melancholy god:* Saturn, whose planet was believed to control people who are easily depressed

74   *doublet:* close-fitting jacket; *changeable taffeta:* a silk woven of many-coloured threads so that its colour seems to change

75   *opal:* a semiprecious gem that, like taffeta, changes colour in different lights

76   *constancy:* Feste is ironic here. He accuses Orsino of *in*constant or changeable behaviour.

78   *makes a . . . nothing:* either "turns *nothing* to any good" or "turns everything to something bad"

80   *give place:* withdraw

81   *yond:* yonder; *sovereign cruelty:* the queen of cruelty

82   *than the world:* than that of any other man in the world

83   *Prizes not:* places no value on

84   *parts:* property, wealth, rank

85   *hold:* value; *giddily:* lightly, indifferently

86   *that miracle . . . gems:* that is, her beauty

87   *pranks her in:* adorns her with

89   *Sooth:* to speak the truth. *I cannot be so answered:* I refuse to accept that answer.

> *Not a friend, not a friend greet*
>   *My poor corpse, where my bones shall*
>   *be thrown.*
> *A thousand thousand sighs to save,*
>   *Lay me, oh, where*
> *Sad true lover never find my grave,*   65
>   *To weep there!*

Duke: There's for thy pains.
Feste: No pains, sir; I take pleasure in singing, sir.
Duke: I'll pay thy pleasure then.
Feste: Truly, sir, and pleasure will be paid, one time or   70
  another.
Duke: Give me now leave to leave thee.
Feste: Now, the melancholy god protect thee; and the
  tailor make thy doublet of changeable taffeta, for
  thy mind is a very opal. I would have men of such   75
  constancy put to sea, that their business might be
  everything and their intent everywhere; for that's
  it that always makes a good voyage of nothing.
  Farewell.
                                    [*Exit.*]
Duke: Let all the rest give place.
                        [*Curio and Attendants retire.*]
                              Once more, Cesario,   80
  Get thee to yond same sovereign cruelty.
  Tell her, my love, more noble than the world,
  Prizes not quantity of dirty lands;
  The parts that fortune hath bestow'd upon her,
  Tell her, I hold as giddily as fortune;   85
  But 'tis that miracle and queen of gems,
  That nature pranks her in, attracts my soul.
Viola: But if she cannot love you, sir?
Duke: I cannot be so answer'd.
Viola: Sooth, but you must.
  Say that some lady, as perhaps there is,   90
  Hath for your love as great a pang of heart
  As you have for Olivia. You cannot love her;
  You tell her so; must she not then be answer'd?
Duke: There is no woman's sides

95   *bide:* withstand, suffer

97   *retention:* a medical term, referring to the ability of the body to retain solids and fluids. Metaphorically, Orsino is speaking of a woman's lack of constancy or intensity in love.

99   *motion:* emotion; *liver, but the palate:* True love is a passion of the liver. Infatuation is a passing hunger.

100   *surfeit, cloyment and revolt:* After overeating (surfeit), the appetite is sickened by even the thought of food (cloyment) and experiences a kind of revulsion (revolt) for it.

112   *concealment:* secrecy

113   *damask:* pink and white like a damask rose; *pined:* wasted away

115   *patience on a monument:* a figure representing patience carved in stone, as on a tomb

118   *Our shows . . . will:* We display more emotion than we really feel; *still:* always

123   *shall I:* shall I go; *theme:* business

125   *can give no place:* may not be prevented, will not yield; *bide no denay:* accept no refusal

Suffer

Can bide the beating of so strong a passion   95
As love doth give my heart; no woman's heart
So big, to hold so much. They lack retention.
Alas, their love may be called appetite,—
No motion of the liver, but the palate,—   Infatuation
That suffer surfeit, cloyment and revolt;   is a passing hunger.
But mine is all as hungry as the sea,
And can digest as much. Make no compare
Between that love a woman can bear me
And that I owe Olivia.

Viola: Ay, but I know—
Duke: What dost thou know?   105
Viola: Too well what love women to men may owe.
In faith, they are as true of heart as we.   If I
My father had a daughter loved a man,   was a   When a lady
As it might be, perhaps, were I a woman,   girl   loves she
I should your lordship.   I would   over does it.
                                                    love you
Duke: Secrecy   And what's her history?   110
Viola: A blank, my lord. She never told her love,
But let concealment, like a worm i' the bud,   Rose like
Feed on her damask cheek. She pined in thought,   coloured.
And with a green and yellow melancholy   wasted away.
She sat like patience on a monument,   115
Smiling at grief. Was not this love indeed?   Patience carved
We men may say more, swear more; but indeed   in stone
Our shows are more than will; for still we prove
Much in our vows, but little in our love.   always.
Duke: But died thy sister of her love, my boy?   120
Viola: I am all the daughters of my father's house,
And all the brothers too; and yet I know not.
Sir, shall I to this lady?
Duke: Shall I go   Ay, that's the theme. Buisness.
To her in haste; give her this jewel; say,
My love can give no place, bide no denay.   [*Exeunt.*] 125

may not be   except no
prevented   refusal.

Emotion

Act 2, Scene 4: Activities

1. Orsino enjoys philosophizing about love, but sometimes he contradicts himself. Reread the two speeches in which he compares men and women in their capacity to love (lines 29–35 and lines 94–104).
   With a partner or in a small group,
   • find the contradictions in Orsino's "wisdom"
   • consider some reasons why Orsino might be unclear or uncertain about love
   • compare his philosophy of love here with his opening speech in Act 1, Scene 1, lines 1–15. How is this scene consistent with the character of Orsino established at the beginning?
   Share your conclusions with another group. Be sure to include the views of both male and female members of the class.

   Do you agree with any ideas which Orsino expresses? Reflect upon your own "philosophy of love" in a journal entry.

2. Debate in parliamentary style:
   Be it resolved that men are more capable of experiencing true love than are women.

   Before you begin, discuss with your teacher the procedure for conducting formal debates.

3. Do you think that the emotion and the experience of love are the same for both men and women? Explore your thoughts and feelings on this topic in a creative piece (poem, short story, or short script).

4. We know that Viola has fallen in love with Orsino. Reread the scene and think about why Viola might find Orsino appealing. As Viola, write a diary entry confessing your love and explaining why you love him.

For the next scene . . .

Why do some people enjoy practical jokes? What enjoyment do practical jokes provide for you? When might a
practical joke not be funny?

Act 2, Scene 5

In this scene . . .

Sir Toby, with Sir Andrew and Fabian (another of his cronies and a member of Olivia's household), hide behind a bush in Olivia's garden to watch Maria's plot against Malvolio unfold. Malvolio enters, daydreaming about his future with Olivia, to whom he is attracted. The discovery of a love letter, apparently from Olivia to him, seems like a dream come true. As he decides to obey every instruction "to the letter," the listeners congratulate Maria on her excellent trap.

1 *Come thy ways:* come along

2 *scruple:* smallest part

3 *boiled to death with melancholy:* die of dejection

4 *niggardly:* miserly, cheap

5 *sheep-biter:* a dog that bites sheep, a nuisance; *come by:* receive; *shame:* public disgrace

7 *bear-baiting:* This popular Elizabethan sport involved tying a bear to a post and allowing a pack of dogs to torment it.

9 *fool him black and blue:* mock him until he is metaphorically bruised black and blue

11 *An:* if; *pity of our lives:* a pity we should continue to live

13 *my metal of India:* my precious. (Gold was commonly called "the metal of India.")

14 *box-tree:* an evergreen shrub used in garden hedges

15-16 *practising behaviour . . . shadow:* trying out various gestures, using his own shadow on the ground as a kind of mirror

16 *this half-hour:* for the past half hour

18 *contemplative:* self-centred; *Close:* remain close together, stay hidden

21 *tickling:* flattery. Fish were caught by stroking them gently around the gills.

23 *she:* Olivia; *affect:* care for

24 *fancy:* love

24-25 *of/my complexion:* like me

25 *uses:* treats

26 *follows:* serves

28 *overweening rogue:* arrogant, conceited knave

Scene 5

Olivia's garden.

*Enter Sir Toby, Sir Andrew,
and Fabian.*

Come along

Sir Toby: Come thy ways, Signior Fabian. *smallest part.*
Fabian: Nay, I'll come; if I lose a scruple of this sport, let
　　me be boiled to death with melancholy. *die of dejection*
Sir Toby: Wouldst thou not be glad to have the niggardly *cheap*
　　rascally sheep-biter come by some notable shame?　　5
Fabian: I would exult, man. You know, he brought me
　　out o' favour with my lady about a bear-baiting here. *Refers to Malvolio as a bear teasing him.*
Sir Toby: To anger him we'll have the bear again; and
　　we will fool him black and blue. Shall we not, Sir
　　Andrew? *if*　　　　　　　　　　　　10
Sir Andrew: An we do not, it is pity of our lives. *A pity we should continue to live.*
Sir Toby: Here comes the little villain.
　　[*Enter Maria.*] *my precious.*
　　How now, my metal of India! *An evergreen shrub uses in garden hedges*
Maria: Get ye all three into the box-tree. Malvolio's coming
　　down this walk. He has been yonder i' the sun prac- *Walking for the past ½ hour talking to self.*
　　tising behaviour to his own shadow this half-hour.
　　Observe him, for the love of mockery; for I know this
　　letter will make a contemplative idiot of him. Close,
　　in the name of jesting! Lie thou there [*Throws down a
　　letter*]; for here comes the trout that must be caught　20 *Past ½ h.*
　　with tickling. *Flattery (that is how they catch fish)* [*Exit.*] *Stay hidden.*
　　[*Enter Malvolio.*]
Malvolio: 'Tis but fortune; all is fortune. Maria once told *care for.*
　　me she did affect me; and I have heard herself come
　　thus near, that, should she fancy, it should be one of *like me.*
　　my complexion. Besides, she uses me with a more *serves*　　25
　　exalted respect than any one else that follows her. What
　　should I think on't?
Sir Toby: Here's an overweening rogue! *Conceited knave.*

29-30   *turkey-/cock:* male turkey, the self-appointed king of the barnyard; *rogue:* knave

30   *jets:* struts; *advanced plumes:* outspread feathers

31   *'Slight:* by God's light

35   *Pistol him:* Shoot him, or beat him with a pistol.

37   *example:* Malvolio's example of a great woman who married beneath her rank may have been invented by Shakespeare.

38   *yeoman:* attendant, servant

39   *Jezebel:* the proud and wicked wife of Ahab, King of Israel, in the Bible (I and II Kings)

40   *deeply in:* completely caught up in his fantasy

41   *blows:* swells, puffs

43   *state:* chair of state

44   *a stone-bow:* a crossbow that shoots stones rather than arrows

45   *branched:* embroidered with a pattern of branches and leaves

46   *day-bed:* couch

50   *to have the humour of the state:* to assume an air of authority and power

51   *demure travel of regard:* a grave look around at my servants

54   *Bolts and shackles:* Sir Toby wishes Malvolio were bound in chains and irons.

56   *start:* jump

56-57   *make/out for him:* go to find him

59   *courtesies:* bows low

61   *Though our . . . cars:* even if we are torn apart by horse-drawn chariots (cars)

64   *familiar:* friendly; *austere regard of control:* stern look of authority

65   *take:* give

68   *prerogative:* right, privilege

Fabian: Oh, peace! Contemplation makes a rare turkey-
cock of him. How he jets under his advanced plumes! 30

Sir Andrew: 'Slight, I could so beat the rogue!

Sir Toby: Peace, I say.

Malvolio: To be Count Malvolio!

Sir Toby: Ah, rogue!

Sir Andrew: Pistol him, pistol him. 35

Sir Toby: Peace, peace!

Malvolio: There is example for't; the lady of the Strachy
married the yeoman of the wardrobe.

Sir Andrew: Fie on him, Jezebel!

Fabian: Oh, peace! now he's deeply in. Look how imagi- 40
nation blows him.

Malvolio: Having been three months married to her, sitting
in my state,—

Sir Toby: Oh, for a stone-bow, to hit him in the eye.

Malvolio: Calling my officers about me, in my branched
velvet gown; having come from a day-bed, where I have
left Olivia sleeping,—

Sir Toby: Fire and brimstone!

Fabian: Oh, peace, peace!

Malvolio: And then to have the humour of state; and after
a demure travel of regard, telling them I know my 50
place as I would they should do theirs, to ask for my
kinsman Toby,—

Sir Toby: Bolts and shackles!

Fabian: O, peace, peace, peace! Now, now. 55

Malvolio: Seven of my people, with an obedient start, make
out for him. I frown the while; and perchance wind
up my watch, or play with my—some rich jewel.
Toby approaches; courtesies there to me,—

Sir Toby: Shall this fellow live? 60

Fabian: Though our silence be drawn from us with cars,
yet peace.

Malvolio: I extend my hand to him thus, quenching my
familiar smile with an austere regard of control,—

Sir Toby: And does not Toby take you a blow o' the lips 65
then?

Malvolio: Saying, "Cousin Toby, my fortunes having cast
me on your niece give me this prerogative of speech,"—

71   *scab:* rotten fellow

72   *break the sinews of:* destroy, disable

73   *treasure of your time:* your valuable time

78   *employment:* business

79   *woodcock:* a proverbially stupid bird; *gin:* trap, snare

80   *the spirit of humours:* whim; *intimate:* suggest

82   *hand:* handwriting

84   *great:* capital; *in contempt of question:* beyond a doubt

85   *Why that?:* Andrew has obviously missed the vulgar jokes.

87   *By your leave, wax:* excuse me for breaking the wax seal on the letter: *Soft:* hold on, not so fast

88   *impressure:* imprint, seal; *Lucrece:* Olivia's ring-seal depicts Lucretia, a noble Roman woman, who stabbed herself after she was raped by Tarquinius. She is symbolic of chastity.

88-89   *uses/to seal:* is accustomed to seal

90   *liver and all:* completely, including his passions

95-96   *The numbers/altered:* in a different rhythm

98   *brock:* badger

100   *like a Lucrece knife:* like the knife with which Lucretia slew herself

103   *fustian:* ridiculous, foolish

Sir Toby: What, what?

Malvolio: "You must amend your drunkenness."

Sir Toby: Out, scab!

Fabian: Nay, patience, or we break the sinews of our plot.

Malvolio: "Besides, you waste the treasure of your time
    with a foolish knight,"—

Sir Andrew: That's me, I warrant you.

Malvolio: "One Sir Andrew,"—

Sir Andrew: I knew 'twas I; for many do call me fool.

Malvolio: What employment have we here?

                                [*Taking up the letter.*]

Fabian: Now is the woodcock near the gin.

Sir Toby: Oh, peace! And the spirit of humours intimate
    reading aloud to him!

Malvolio: By my life, this is my lady's hand. These be her
    very C's, her U's, and her T's; and thus makes she
    her great P's. It is, in contempt of question, her hand.

Sir Andrew: Her C's, her U's, and her T's. Why that?

Malvolio: [*Reads.*] *To the unknown beloved, this, and my good*
    wishes:—her very phrases! By your leave, wax. Soft!
    And the impressure her Lucrece, with which she uses
    to seal. 'Tis my lady. To whom should this be?

Fabian: This wins him liver and all.

Malvolio: [*Reads.*]

    Jove knows I love;
        But who?
        Lips, do not move;
        No man must know.

    "No man must know." What follows? The numbers
    altered.

    "No man must know"—if this should be thee, Malvolio?

Sir Toby: Marry, hang thee, brock!

Malvolio: [*Reads.*]

    I may command where I adore;
      But silence, like a Lucrece knife,
    With bloodless stroke my heart doth gore.
      M, O, A, I, doth sway my life.

Fabian: A fustian riddle!

Sir Toby: Excellent wench, say I.

70

75

80

85

90

95

100

107   *dressed him?:* prepared him for

108   *with what . . . it:* with what speed *(wing)* the sparrow hawk *(staniel)* turns to snatch at the prey

111   *formal capacity:* normal intelligence; *obstruction:* problem, difficulty

113   *position:* arrangement

115   *make up that:* work that out; *at a cold scent:* not recognizing the scent of the animal he's hunting

116   *Sowter will cry upon't:* Sowter (a common name for a foxhound) will recognize the scent of the hunted animal and howl. (Even though the trick is as obvious as the smell of a fox to a hound, Fabian realizes that Malvolio has been caught.)

120   *faults:* breaks in the scent

121   *consonancy:* consistency; *sequel:* sequence

122   *that suffers under probation:* The sequence is not correct when it is tested.

124   *O shall end:* Malvolio's howl of embarrassment and shame when he discovers the joke

125   *cudgel:* beat

126   *behind:* at the end

128   *detraction at your heels:* bad luck behind you

130   *simulation:* hidden meaning, puzzle

131   *crush:* force; *bow:* point

134   *revolve:* reflect, think; *stars:* fortune

137   *open their hands:* in a gesture of welcome and support

138   *inure:* accustom

139   *cast thy humble slough:* cast off your humility

140   *opposite with:* hostile to

141   *tang arguments of state:* resound with important matters of politics; *surly:* rude

141-142 *trick of/singularity:* affectations of eccentricity

144   *ever:* always; *cross-gartered:* with garters crossed both above and below the knee; *Go to:* come on

Malvolio: "M, O, A, I, doth sway my life." Nay, but first, 105
  let me see, let me see, let me see.
Fabian: What dish o' poison has she dressed him?
Sir Toby: And with what wing the staniel checks at it!
Malvolio: "I may command where I adore." Why she may
  command me: I serve her; she is my lady. Why, this 110
  is evident to any formal capacity; there is no obstruction
  in this. And the end,—what should that alphabetical
  position portend? If I could make that resemble
  something in me,—Softly! M, O, A, I,—
Sir Toby: Oh, ay, make up that; he is now at a cold scent. 115
Fabian: Sowter will cry upon't for all this, though it be
  as rank as a fox.
Malvolio: M,—Malvolio; M,—why, that begins my name.
Fabian: Did not I say he would work it out? The cur is
  excellent at faults.
Malvolio: M,—but then there is no consonancy in the sequel; 120
  that suffers under probation. A should follow, but O
  does.
Fabian: And O shall end, I hope.
Sir Toby: Ay, or I'll cudgel him, and make him cry O! 125
Malvolio: And then I comes behind.
Fabian: Ay, an you had an eye behind you, you might see
  more detraction at your heels than fortunes before
  you.
Malvolio: M, O, A, I. This simulation is not as the former; 130
  and yet, to crush this a little, it would bow to me, for
  every one of these letters are in my name. Soft! here
  follows prose.
  [*Reads.*] *If this fall into thy hand, revolve. In my stars I
  am above thee; but be not afraid of greatness: some are born* 135
  great, some achieve greatness, and some have greatness
  thrust upon 'em. Thy fates open their hands; let thy blood
  and spirit embrace them; and, to inure thyself to what
  thou art like to be, cast thy humble slough and appear fresh.
  Be opposite with a kinsman, surly with servants; let thy 140
  tongue tang arguments of state; put thyself into the trick of
  singularity. She thus advises thee that sighs for thee.
  Remember who commended thy yellow stockings, and
  wished to see thee ever cross-gartered. I say, remember.

115

145   *thou art made:* Your fortune is made.

146   *still:* always

148   *alter services:* change positions (so that Malvolio would be her lord and master)

150   *champain:* open country; *discovers:* reveals

151   *open:* clear, unmistakeable; *politic authors:* books on politics and government

152   *baffle:* treat with contempt; *wash off:* cast aside

153   *point-devise:* exactly, precisely; *gross acquaintance:* vulgar companions

154   *jade:* deceive

154-155   *every reason/excites to this:* Every piece of evidence points to this fact.

156   *of late:* recently

158   *injunction:* command

159   *habits:* clothes; *manifests:* shows

160   *strange:* distant, aloof; *stout:* proud

161-162   *even with . . . on:* as quickly as I can put them on

165   *entertainest:* accept

166   *become:* suit; *still:* always

171   *the Sophy:* the Shah of Persia (noted for his wealth and generosity)

177   *gull-catcher:* fool-catcher

178   *Wilt thou . . . neck?:* Because Maria has been victorious, Toby invites her to pin him to the ground with her foot on his neck. This was the traditional position of a conqueror and a defeated victim.

180   *play:* gamble, risk; *tray-trip:* game of dice in which threes (trays) had to be thrown

Go to, thou art made, if thou desirest to be so; if not, let   145
me see thee a steward still, the fellow of servants, and
not worthy to touch Fortune's fingers. Farewell. She that
would alter services with thee,

                                        The Fortunate Unhappy.

Daylight and champain discovers not more. This is   150
open. I will be proud, I will read politic authors, I will
baffle Sir Toby, I will wash off gross acquaintance;
I will be point-devise the very man. I do not now fool
myself, to let imagination jade me; for every reason
excites to this, that my lady loves me. She did com-   155
mend my yellow stockings of late, she did praise my leg
being cross-gartered; and in this she manifests herself
to my love, and with a kind of injunction drives me
to these habits of her liking. I thank my stars I am
happy. I will be strange, stout, in yellow stockings, and   160
cross-gartered, even with the swiftness of putting
on. Jove and my stars be praised! Here is yet a
postscript.

    [*Reads.*] *Thou canst not choose but know who I am. If*
thou entertainest my love, let it appear in thy smiling. Thy   165
smiles become thee well; therefore in my presence still
smile, dear my sweet, I prithee.

    Jove, I thank thee. I will smile; I will do everything
    that thou wilt have me.   [*Exit.*]

Fabian: I will not give my part of this sport for a pension   170
    of thousands to be paid from the Sophy.
Sir Toby: I could marry this wench for this device.
Sir Andrew: So could I too.
Sir Toby: And ask no other dowry with her but such another
    jest.   175
Sir Andrew: Nor I neither.
Fabian: Here comes my noble gull-catcher.
    [*Re-enter Maria.*]
Sir Toby: Wilt thou set thy foot o' my neck?
Sir Andrew: Or o' mine either?
Sir Toby: Shall I play my freedom at tray-trip, and become   180
    thy bond-slave?
Sir Andrew: I' faith, or I either?

186   *aqua vitæ:* brandy or other distilled liqueurs; *midwife:* a woman
      who assists in the delivery of babies

187   *fruits of the sport:* the final results of our trick

193   *notable contempt:* notorious object of scorn and contempt

195   *Tartar:* Tartarus, the underworld in classical mythology

197   *make one:* come along

Sir Toby: Why, thou hast put him in such a dream, that
   when the image of it leaves him he must run mad.

Maria: Nay, but say true: does it work upon him?   185

Sir Toby: Like aqua vitae with a midwife.

Maria: If you will then see the fruits of the sport, mark his
   first approach before my lady. He will come to her
   in yellow stockings, and 'tis a colour she abhors; and
   cross-gartered, a fashion she detests; and he will smile   190
   upon her, which will now be so unsuitable to her disposition, being addicted to a melancholy as she is,
   that it cannot but turn him into a notable contempt.
   If you will see it, follow me.

Sir Toby: To the gates of Tartar, thou most excellent devil   195
   of wit!

Sir Andrew: I'll make one too.   [*Exeunt.*]

Act 2, Scene 5: Activities

1. a) In a group of four, explore some different ways of portraying characters in this scene.
   - Reread lines 21–169. How would you get an audience to support Malvolio and not Sir Toby? Consider how the lines would be spoken and how the actors would move and behave.
   - How could the same lines be presented so that the audience would side with Toby, not Malvolio?
   - Is it possible to play this section so that neither Malvolio nor Toby deserves the audience's sympathy?

   b) Prepare a reading of all or part of the section, choosing one of the three ways – sympathetic to Malvolio, sympathetic to Toby, sympathetic to neither character – of presenting the material. Perform your dramatization live or videotape it for the class. Have the audience explain how they responded to the different characters.

   c) When all three dramatic readings have been performed, write a director's log entry in which you defend one of the interpretations as being the most suitable. Compare and discuss your choice with others.

2. As Malvolio, write a diary entry in which you reveal your feelings and develop your plan, now that you have discovered Olivia's love. Your diary entry might include poetry about Olivia.

3. This scene, like all of those in which Sir Toby and his cronies appear, contains many words and phrases that are the colloquial language or slang of Shakespeare's time. Rewrite the opening twenty lines of this scene in modern English, replacing the colloquialisms with language you and your friends would use. You might experiment with different settings.

Share your rewrite for another group, asking them to comment on how well you captured the atmosphere of the scene.

Act 2: Consider the Whole Act

1. a) Malvolio's official position as steward of the household makes him a likely candidate for satirical treatment. Where else have you seen a "Malvolio" — a strict bureaucrat or authority figure? In a small group, generate a list of examples from books you have read and from plays and movies you have seen. Share your list with the rest of the class.

   b) Select one of the characters and improvise a dramatic scene in which the character is ridiculed or satirized. You could place the character in a scene you re-create from this Act or create a new scene.

   After your presentation, explain to the class what kind of person you were satirizing. Ask your audience how effectively they thought the satire was developed.

2. Sebastian and Antonio have appeared only once. In a journal entry, suggest what they have been doing since we saw them last and predict how they may become involved in the plot of the play.

3. "Dost thou think, because thou art virtuous, there shall be no more cakes and ale?" (Scene 3, lines 108–109)

   Sir Toby and Malvolio represent opposite extremes in their attitudes towards life, and each is intolerant of the other's point of view. What point of view does each character represent? Which philosophy of life do you find more disturbing? Why? Write a letter to one of these characters, offering your advice on how he might live a fuller life.

4. In Scene 4, line 17, Orsino proclaims, "For such as I am all true lovers are."
Debate in parliamentary style:
Be it resolved that Orsino provides an excellent model of the "true lover."

5. Sir Toby and his friends play a practical joke on Malvolio. Have you or someone you know ever tried to teach a friend a lesson by playing a practical joke? Did the joke have the intended effect? Were there unexpected consequences? Would you do it again? Why or why not? Share your stories and comments with a small group. Consider creating a short story or improvisation based on one of the stories for presentation to the class. List the different ways the joke might have ended. Use them to provide a variety of endings for your scene.

6. Write a letter to Shakespeare in which you ask questions and make comments about the play to this point. Consider these beginnings as a guide:
   • Why did you . . .?
   • Why didn't you . . .?
   • I really like the way you . . .
   • I do not understand . . .
   • I do not like . . .
   Exchange letters with a partner. As Shakespeare, compose a letter in response to your partner's questions. Perhaps the class could discuss some of the more difficult or interesting questions.

For the next scene . . .

Why might it be difficult to break away from accepted or expected behaviour? Have you ever done something that was different from what most people do? If so, what were the results?

Act 3, Scene 1

In this scene . . .

Viola returns to Olivia's house, ready to resume her courtship of Olivia on Orsino's behalf. In the garden, she meets Feste and engages in a brief battle of wits with him. When Feste leaves to summon Olivia, Viola has a short conversation with Sir Toby and Sir Andrew. Olivia enters and immediately dismisses the others so that she and Cesario can be alone. Once again rejecting Orsino's offers of love, she openly reveals her affection for Cesario. Viola expresses only pity for Olivia's feelings and swears that she will never love a woman.

Stage direction – *tabor:* small drum

1   *Save thee:* God save you; *live by:* earn your living with. Feste
     takes the expression to mean "live near."

4   *churchman:* preacher

6   *by:* near

8   *lies by:* sleeps with or dwells near

9   *stands by:* is supported by, or is situated near

11   *To see this age:* what times we live in; *sentence:* wise saying,
     proverb

12   *cheveril:* kid leather

14   *dally:* play; *nicely:* making precise distinctions in meaning

15   *wanton:* ambiguous in meaning. (Feste takes the word to mean
     loose or unchaste.)

16   *I would . . . name:* I wish that my sister had not been given a
     name.

21   *words are very rascals:* words cannot be trusted

21-22 *since bonds/disgraced them:* Ever since written agreements
       (*bonds*) were introduced to guarantee a person's prom-
       ises, words themselves have been cheapened (*disgraced*)
       and considered unreliable.

24   *Troth:* to tell the truth; *yield:* give

25   *I am loath:* I am unwilling

27   *warrant:* believe; *car'st for:* care about

Act 3, Scene 1

Olivia's garden.

*Enter Viola, and Feste with
a tabor.*

*[Handwritten: Coherance by
Act 1 scene 1
Act 3 scene 1]*

[Handwritten: God Save you]

[Handwritten margin: Punning]

Viola: Save thee, friend, and thy music. Dost thou live by
thy tabor? *[Handwritten: small drum. Earn your living by.]*
Feste: No, sir, I live by the church.
Viola: Art thou a churchman? *[Handwritten: Preacher]*
Feste: No such matter, sir. I do live by the church; for I   5
do live at my house, and my house doth stand by the *[Handwritten: near]* *[Handwritten: Supported by.]*
church.
Viola: So thou mayst say, the king lies by a beggar, if a *[Handwritten: sleeps with/dwells near.]*
beggar dwell near him; or, the church stands by thy
tabor, if thy tabor stand by the church. *[Handwritten: live in.]*   10
Feste: You have said, sir. To see this age! A sentence is *[Handwritten: What times we live in.]*
but a cheveril glove to a good wit. How quickly the *[Handwritten: kid leather]* *[Handwritten: proverb.]*
wrong side may be turned outward!
Viola: Nay, that's certain. They that dally nicely with words *[Handwritten: distinctly.]*
may quickly make them wanton. *[Handwritten: Ambiguous in meaning.]*
Feste: I would, therefore, my sister had had no name,   15
sir. *[Handwritten: I wish my sister was never given a name.]*
Viola: Why, man?
Feste: Why, sir, her name's a word; and to dally with
that word might make my sister wanton. But   20
indeed words are very rascals since bonds *[Handwritten: words cant be trusted]*
disgraced them.
Viola: Thy reason, man? *[Handwritten: To tell truth since]*
Feste: Troth, sir, I can yield you none without words; and
words are grown so false, I am loath to prove reason *[Handwritten: I am unwilling]*   25
with them. *[Handwritten: believe]*
Viola: I warrant thou art a merry fellow and carest for *[Handwritten: Care about]*
nothing.

127

29-30 *in my/conscience:* truthfully

36 *pilchards:* small herrings

39 *late:* recently

41 *but:* unless

41-42 *but the . . . mistress:* Feste's comment here has two meanings: "I enjoy the company of your master as much as I enjoy the company of my mistress" and "your master is as big a fool as my mistress."

43 *your wisdom:* you. Compare to the expression "your highness."

44 *an thou pass upon me:* if you make fun of me; *I'll no more with thee:* I won't speak with you any longer.

46 *commodity:* supply, assignment

51 *a pair of these:* i.e., two coins; *bred:* multiplied (given birth to others)

52 *put to use:* invested. (Viola may or may not have caught Feste's sexual joke.)

53-54 *I would . . . Troilus:* Troilus, a Trojan prince, and Cressida, the daughter of a Greek priest, were famous lovers during the Trojan War. Cressida's uncle, Pandarus, had introduced the two and helped them to meet secretly. As Pandarus, Feste hopes to receive a second coin (Cressida) as a match for the one (Troilus) he has already received from Viola.

57 *Cressida was a beggar:* In some versions of the story, Cressida becomes a leper and is forced to beg for a living.

58 *construe:* explain

59 *welkin:* sky

59-60 *I might/ . . . overworn: Welkin* and *element* are synonymous. Feste has avoided the phrase *out of my element* (beyond my knowledge) because it had become a cliche.

62 *craves:* requires

63 *their mood . . . jests:* the mood of the people he is entertaining

64 *quality:* social status and/or character

65 *haggard:* untrained hawk

65-66 *check at . . . eye:* swoop down upon every bird he sees

66 *practice:* skill

Feste: Not so, sir, I do care for something; but in my
conscience, sir, I do not care for you. If that be   30
to care for nothing, sir, I would it would make you
invisible.

Viola: Art not thou the Lady Olivia's fool?

Feste: No, indeed, sir; the Lady Olivia has no folly. She
will keep no fool, sir, till she be married; and fools are   35
as like husbands as pilchards are to herrings; the
husband's the bigger. I am indeed not her fool, but her
corrupter of words.

Viola: I saw thee late at the Count Orsino's.

Feste: Foolery, sir, does walk about the orb like the sun, it 40
shines everywhere. I would be sorry, sir, but the fool
should be as oft with your master as with my mistress.
I think I saw your wisdom there.

Viola: Nay, an thou pass upon me, I'll no more with thee.
Hold, there's expenses for thee.   45

Feste: Now, Jove, in his next commodity of hair, send thee
a beard!

Viola: By my troth, I'll tell thee, I am almost sick for one—
[*Aside.*] though I would not have it grow on my chin.
Is thy lady within?   50

Feste: Would not a pair of these have bred, sir?

Viola: Yes, being kept together, and put to use.

Feste: I would play Lord Pandarus of Phrygia, sir, to bring
a Cressida to this Troilus.

Viola: I understand you, sir, 'tis well begged.   55

                    [*Gives him another coin.*]

Feste: The matter, I hope, is not great, sir, begging but a
beggar: Cressida was a beggar. My lady is within sir. I
will construe to them whence you come. Who you are
and what you would are out of my welkin, I might
say element, but the word is overworn.   [*Exit.*] 60

Viola: This fellow is wise enough to play the fool;
And to do that well craves a kind of wit.
He must observe their mood on whom he jests,
The quality of persons, and the time,
And, like the haggard, check at every feather   65
That comes before his eye. This is a practice
As full of labour as a wise man's art;

68   *fit:* proper, appropriate

69   *folly-fall'n:* fallen into folly; *quite taint their wit:* corrupt their intelligence

70   *Save you:* God save you.

72   *Dieu vous garde, monsieur:* God keep you, sir. Sir Andrew has remembered some of his French!

73   *Et vous aussi; votre serviteur:* And you, too. I am your humble servant.

75   *encounter:* approach, enter

76   *if your . . . her:* if your business is with her

77   *bound to:* headed for. (Viola continues Sir Toby's trading metaphor); *list:* destination

79   *Taste:* try

80   *understand me:* stand under me

83   *with gait and entrance:* by walking and entering

84   *prevented:* hindered, stopped (anticipated?)

87   *well:* well put. (Sir Andrew is impressed with Viola's fancy language.)

88   *My matter hath no voice:* My business cannot be spoken about.

89   *pregnant:* expectant, ready (to hear); *vouchsafed:* attentive

91   *ready:* prepared (for my own use). Andrew would love to be able to use the poetic language of Viola.

98-99   *'Twas never . . . compliment:* The world has been unhappy since false humility was considered an appropriate form of compliment.

101   *yours:* i.e., your servant; *and his must needs be yours:* and what is his must also be yours

103   *For him:* as for him

104   *Would they were blanks:* I wish they were empty.

105   *whet:* sharpen (and make more sensitive to Orsino)

For folly that he wisely shows is fit,
But wise men, folly-fall'n, quite taint their wit.
[*Enter Sir Toby and Sir Andrew.*]
Sir Toby: Save you, gentlemen.   70
Viola: And you, sir.
Sir Andrew: Dieu vous garde, monsieur.
Viola: Et vous aussi, votre serviteur.
Sir Andrew: I hope, sir, you are; and I am yours.
Sir Toby: Will you encounter the house? My niece is desirous   75
   you should enter, if your trade be to her.
Viola: I am bound to your niece, sir; I mean, she is the list
   of my voyage.
Sir Toby: Taste your legs, sir; put them to motion.
Viola: My legs do better understand me, sir, than I under-   80
   stand what you mean by bidding me taste my legs.
Sir Toby: I mean, to go, sir, to enter.
Viola: I will answer you with gait and entrance. But we are
   prevented. [*Enter Olivia and Maria.*] Most excellent
   accomplished lady, the heavens rain odours on you!   85
Sir Andrew: That youth's a rare courtier. "Rain odours",
   well.
Viola: My matter hath no voice, lady, but to your own most
   pregnant and vouchsafed ear.
Sir Andrew: "Odours", "pregnant", and "vouchsafed". I'll   90
   get 'em all three all ready.
Olivia: Let the garden door be shut, and leave me to my
   hearing. [*Exeunt Sir Toby, Sir Andrew, and Maria.*] Give
   me your hand, sir.
Viola: My duty, madam, and most humble service.   95
Olivia: What is your name?
Viola: Cesario is your servant's name, fair princess.
Olivia: My servant, sir! 'Twas never merry world
   Since lowly feigning was call'd compliment.
   You're servant to the Count Orsino, youth.   100
Viola: And he is yours, and his must needs be yours.
   Your servant's servant is your servant, madam.
Olivia: For him, I think not on him; for his thoughts,
   Would they were blanks, rather than fill'd with me!
Viola: Madam, I come to whet your gentle thoughts   105
   On his behalf.

131

109   *solicit:* argue for

110   *music from the spheres:* Elizabethans believed that the planets and stars created music that could be heard by God and his angels, but not by human ears.

113   *abuse:* malign, insult; *cunning:* trick

115   *hard construction:* severe judgement

116   *that:* i.e., the ring; *cunning:* trick

117   *none of yours:* did not belong to you

118-120 *Have you . . . think?:* The extended metaphor here compares Oliva's honour to a bear tied to the stake and tormented (*baited*) by dogs (Viola's *thoughts*). The thoughts, being *unmuzzled*, are dangerous.

121   *cypress:* not the tree, but a thin black veil worn by female mourners

123   *degree to:* step towards

124   *grize:* step; *vulgar proof:* common knowledge

126   *Why, then . . . again:* If that's true, I think I'd better try to overcome love's sadness

127   *how apt . . . proud:* The unfortunate and rejected (*poor*) are always ready (*apt*) to be proud of their distress.

132   *when wit . . . harvest:* when you are mature

133   *like:* likely; *proper:* handsome, worthy

135   *Grace:* the blessing of God; *good disposition:* peace of mind

136   *You'll nothing . . . me?:* Have you nothing you wish me to take to my master?

139   *That you . . . are:* Viola's answer is intentionally ambiguous. Her meaning could be "You think that you are in love with a man, but you are not."

140   *If I . . . you:* Olivia thinks that Viola has accused her of forgetting her social rank and acting beneath herself. This response indicates her belief that Cesario too has mistaken his proper rank and is more worthy and noble than he believes himself to be.

141   *what I am:* what I appear to be

Olivia: Oh, by your leave, I pray you,
I bade you never speak again of him;
But, would you undertake another suit,
I had rather hear you to solicit that
Than music from the spheres.

Viola: Dear lady,—   110

Olivia: Give me leave, beseech you. I did send,
After the last enchantment you did here,
A ring in chase of you; so did I abuse
Myself, my servant, and, I fear me, you.
Under your hard construction must I sit,   115
To force that on you, in a shameful cunning,
Which you knew none of yours. What might you think?
Have you not set mine honour at the stake
And baited it with all the unmuzzled thoughts
That tyrannous heart can think? To one of your receiving   120
Enough is shown. A cypress, not a bosom,
Hideth my heart. So, let me hear you speak.

Viola: I pity you.

Olivia: That's a degree to love.

Viola: No, not a grize; for 'tis a vulgar proof,
That very oft we pity enemies.   125

Olivia: Why, then, methinks 'tis time to smile again.
O world, how apt the poor are to be proud!
If one should be a prey, how much the better
To fall before the lion than the wolf!

                              [*Clock strikes.*]

The clock upbraids me with the waste of time.   130
Be not afraid, good youth, I will not have you;
And yet, when wit and youth is come to harvest,
Your wife is like to reap a proper man.
There lies your way, due west.

Viola: Then westward-ho!
Grace and good disposition attend your ladyship!   135
You'll nothing, madam, to my lord by me?

Olivia: Stay.
I prithee, tell me what thou think'st of me.

Viola: That you do think you are not what you are.

Olivia: If I think so, I think the same of you.   140

Viola: Then think you right; I am not what I am.

142   *I would . . . be:* I wish you were what I would like you to be.

144   *I am your fool:* You are making a fool of me.

145-146 *Oh, what . . . lip:* How attractive scorn and contempt can be when they are expressed in his angry lip!

147   *A murderous guilt:* the crime of murder

148   *love that would seem hid:* love that tries to remain secret; *Love's night is noon:* Love, even when it tries to remain secret, is as clear as day.

151   *maugre:* in spite of pride (as displayed in the *anger* of line 146)

152   *Nor wit nor reason:* neither intelligence nor common sense

153-156 *Do not . . . better:* Do not persuade yourself (*extort thy reasons*) that, just because I am the wooer, you have no reason to accept and return my love. Instead, oppose the previous argument with the one that follows.

159   *no woman has:* i.e., Viola has not promised her heart to any woman.

160   *save:* except

162   *deplore:* pour out

163   *move:* persuade, convince

Olivia: I would you were as I would have you be!

Viola: Would it be better, madam, than I am?
I wish it might, for now I am your fool.

Olivia: Oh, what a deal of scorn looks beautiful
In the contempt and anger of his lip!
A murderous guilt shows not itself more soon
Than love that would seem hid. Love's night is noon.
Cesario, by the roses of the spring,
By maidhood, honour, truth and everything,
I love thee so, that, maugre all thy pride,
Nor wit nor reason can my passion hide.
Do not extort thy reasons from this clause,
For that I woo, thou therefore hast no cause;
But rather reason thus with reason fetter;
Love sought is good, but given unsought is better.

Viola: By innocence I swear, and by my youth,
I have one heart, one bosom and one truth,
And that no woman has; nor never none
Shall mistress be of it, save I alone.
And so adieu, good madam. Never more
Will I my master's tears to you deplore.

Olivia: Yet come again; for thou perhaps mayest move
That heart, which now abhors, to like his love. [*Exeunt.*]

Handwritten annotations:
- I wish you were what I want you to be.
- you're making a fool of me.
- He is beautiful even when he is mad.
- Crime of murder
- motives to remain hidden / secret. when secret it is clear.
- rhyming couplet
- in spite of pride
- intelligent common sense.
- Couplet
- Couplet
- Couplet — Paradox
- couplet
- Viola has not promised her heart to any woman.
- except
- visual rhyming couplet?
- persuade. / couplet / poor art
- Visual, Rhyming couplet?
- Almost all lines except the first 4 lines are rhyming couplets.
- Dramatic Irony.

145

150

155

160

Act 3, Scene 1: Activities

1. "They that dally nicely with words may quickly make them wanton." (lines 14–15)
   At the beginning of this scene, Feste and Viola agree that words are ambiguous and, if used cleverly, may be very deceiving.

   a) How does this warning apply to the rest of the scene? Consider Aguecheek's admiration of Cesario and the courtship scene between Olivia and Cesario. Share your ideas in a small group.

   b) How does this warning apply today? Consider the clever or ambiguous use of words by politicians and advertisers (in advertising, for example, "fresh" and "natural"; in politics, "democratic" and "free"). Compose a short political speech in which you use words in this way to appeal to the values and prejudices of a specific audience. As an alternative, create an advertisement which makes a product sound attractive without giving any information about it or an ad that "sells" a useless or unattractive product.

2. In this courtship scene, neither Olivia nor Viola behaves as she did in Act 1, Scene 5. With a partner, compare the two meetings between Olivia and Cesario/Viola. Read aloud Act 1, Scene 5, lines 161–278, and this scene, lines 93–164. Discuss the ways in which both characters have changed. Consider the following:
   • Viola's behaviour with her "superior"
   • her attitude towards Olivia's predicament
   • Olivia's adherence to the rules of courtship

3. In Shakespeare's play *A Midsummer Night's Dream*, Helena, who is one of the unhappy heroines in the play, laments the woman's role in courtship:

"We cannot fight for love, as men may do;
We should be woo'd and were not made to woo."

Olivia is obviously bold enough to reject this convention.

- In a journal entry, record your own feelings about the
  traditional "roles" of males and females in dating
  and courtship. Be sure to consider why these roles
  exist and whether you approve of them.
- In a small group, share your thoughts, and try to devise
  a *new* code of dating behaviour that your group
  can agree upon.

For the next scene . . .

How do boys try to have girls notice them today? How do
you think they might have attracted the attention of girls
in Shakespeare's day?

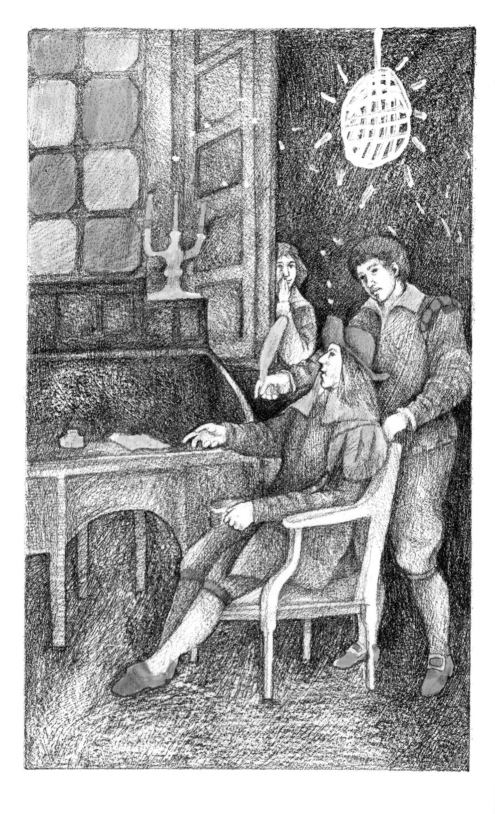

Act 3, Scene 2

In this scene . . .

Sir Andrew has seen Cesario and Olivia together in the garden and has decided, once again, to abandon his courtship of Olivia. Sir Toby and Fabian convince Andrew that Olivia was friendly with Cesario only to make Andrew jealous. They encourage him to challenge Cesario to a duel, arguing that courage is the best way to win a woman's heart. Maria enters to reveal that Malvolio has fallen completely into their trap and is wandering around the house in yellow, cross-gartered stockings with a huge smile on his face. Together, they run off to see the fun.

1   *jot:* moment

2   *dear venom:* sweet poison

3   *yield:* reveal

4   *Marry:* indeed

7   *the while:* at the same time

9   *great argument:* strong proof

12   *legitimate:* correct; *upon the oaths of:* according to the testimony of

14   *grand-jurymen:* expert witnesses

14-15 *since before . . . sailor:* since before the Flood (Genesis, chapters 6-8)

17   *dormouse valour:* minimal courage (as much as a very small mouse might have)

18   *brimstone:* sulphur, the fuel of hell-fire; *fire in . . . liver:* The heart and the liver were the seats of courage, as well as love.

19   *accosted:* approached, confronted

20   *fire-new from the mint:* like shining coins that have just been minted

21-22 *looked for/at your hand:* expected of you

22   *balked:* neglected, refused; *double gilt:* extra thick layer of gold. (Sir Andrew has missed a golden opportunity.)

24   *into the . . . opinion:* i.e., out of the warmth of her favour and into the cold

25   *like an icicle on a Dutchman's beard:* Probably an allusion to the Arctic voyage (1596-97) of William Barents, a Dutchman whose adventures were published just before *Twelfth Night* was written.

26   *laudable attempt:* notable effort

27   *valour or policy:* courage or diplomacy. Sir Andrew takes *policy* to mean trickery or deceit.

29   *I had as lief:* I would rather; *Brownist:* followers of Robert Brown, who advocated the complete separation of church and state. Sir Andrew probably uses the term as a synonym for Puritan; *politician:* schemer

Scene 2

A room in Olivia's house.

*Enter Sir Toby, Sir Andrew, and
Fabian.*

Sir Andrew: No, faith, I'll not stay a jot longer.
Sir Toby: Thy reason, dear venom, give thy reason.
Fabian: You must needs yield your reason, Sir Andrew.
Sir Andrew: Marry, I saw your niece do more favours to the
    count's serving-man than ever she bestowed upon   5
    me. I saw't i' the orchard.
Sir Toby: Did she see thee the while, old boy? Tell me that.
Sir Andrew: As plain as I see you now.
Fabian: This was a great argument of love in her toward
    you.   10
Sir Andrew: Will you make an ass o' me?
Fabian: I will prove it legitimate, sir, upon the oaths of
    judgement and reason.
Sir Toby: And they have been grand-jurymen since before
    Noah was a sailor.   15
Fabian: She did show favour to the youth in your sight only
    to exasperate you, to awake your dormouse valour,
    to put fire in your heart, and brimstone in your liver.
    You should then have accosted her; and with some
    excellent jests, fire-new from the mint, you should have   20
    banged the youth into dumbness. This was looked for
    at your hand, and this was balked. The double gilt of
    this opportunity you let time wash off, and you are
    now sailed into the north of my lady's opinion, where
    you will hang like an icicle on a Dutchman's beard,   25
    unless you do redeem it by some laudable attempt either
    of valour or policy.
Sir Andrew: An't be any way, it must be with valour; for
    policy I hate. I had as lief be a Brownist as a politician.

30   *build me:* I suggest that you build

34-35   *can more . . . woman:* that can have a bigger effect upon a woman's positive opinion of a man

38   *curst:* fierce, bold

40   *invention:* brilliance; *with the licence of ink:* with the freedom that writing allows (i.e., Sir Andrew's accusations would be more risky if spoken directly to Viola/Cesario.)

40-41   *If thou/thou'st him:* if you call him *thou.* (*Thou,* as opposed to *you,* was usually used to address intimate friends or social inferiors.)

41   *thrice:* three times; *it shall not be amiss:* It would not be a bad idea.

43   *bed of Ware:* a famous bed, reputed to sleep up to twelve people

45   *gall enough:* sufficient bitterness

48   *cubiculo:* little room

49   *dear manakin:* sweet puppet

50   *dear to him:* Toby puns on the meaning of *dear* as expensive and he means, "I have cost him."

50-51   *some two thousand/strong:* two thousand ducats or so

54   *by all means:* using every possible trick; *stir on:* provoke

55   *wainropes:* heavy ropes used to pull wagons

56   *hale:* haul, drag

59   *opposite:* opponent; *visage:* face

60   *presage:* indication

62   *desire the spleen:* The spleen was considered to be the controller of laughter.

63   *Yond gull:* that fool

65   *that means . . . rightly:* who hopes to be saved from damnation by believing in the teachings of Christianity

66   *impossible passages of grossness:* extreme improbabilities (i.e., the commands in the letter)

Sir Toby: Why, then, build me thy fortunes upon the basis 30
of valour. Challenge me the count's youth to fight
with him; hurt him in eleven places. My niece shall
take note of it; and assure thyself, there is no love-
broker in the world can more prevail in man's com-
mendation with woman than report of valour. 35

Fabian: There is no way but this, Sir Andrew.

Sir Andrew: Will either of you bear me a challenge to him?

Sir Toby: Go, write it in a martial hand; be curst and brief;
it is no matter how witty, so it be eloquent and full of
invention. Taunt him with the licence of ink. If thou 40
thou'st him some thrice, it shall not be amiss; and as
many lies as will lie in thy sheet of paper, although
the sheet were big enough for the bed of Ware in
England, set 'em down. Go, about it. Let there be
gall enough in thy ink; though thou write with a goose- 45
pen, no matter. About it.

Sir Andrew: Where shall I find you?

Sir Toby: We'll call thee at the cubiculo. Go.

[*Exit Sir Andrew.*]

Fabian: This is a dear manakin to you, Sir Toby.

Sir Toby: I have been dear to him, lad, some two thousand 50
strong, or so.

Fabian: We shall have a rare letter from him; but you'll
not deliver't?

Sir Toby: Never trust me, then; and by all means stir on
the youth to an answer. I think oxen and wainropes 55
cannot hale them together. For Andrew, if he were
opened, and you find so much blood in his liver as will
clog the foot of a flea, I'll eat the rest of the anatomy.

Fabian: And his opposite, the youth, bears in his visage
no great presage of cruelty. 60

[*Enter Maria.*]

Sir Toby: Look, where the youngest wren of nine comes.

Maria: If you desire the spleen, and will laugh yourselves
into stitches, follow me. Yond gull Malvolio is turned
heathen, a very renegado; for there is no Christian,
that means to be saved by believing rightly, can ever 65
believe such impossible passages of grossness. He's
in yellow stockings.

69-70　*like a . . . church:* like a strict schoolmaster who teaches in a church because he has no school

70　*dogged him, like his murderer:* followed him closely as if I intended to murder him

73　*augmentation:* addition

74　*Indies:* the islands of the South Pacific. A new map of the world, prepared in 1599 or 1600, that showed more detail of the far East than any previous map.

75　*forbear:* prevent myself

76　*take't for:* consider it to be

Sir Toby: And cross-gartered?

Maria: Most villainously, like a pedant that keeps a school
i' the church. I have dogged him, like his murderer.
He does obey every point of the letter that I dropped
to betray him. He does smile his face into more lines
than is in the new map with the augmentation of the
Indies; you have not seen such a thing as 'tis. I can
hardly forbear hurling things at him. I know my lady, 75
will strike him. If she do, he'll smile and take 't for
a great favour.

Sir Toby: Come, bring us, bring us where he is.   [*Exeunt.*]

Act 3, Scene 2: Activities

1. At the beginning of this scene, Sir Andrew has decided to return home. As Sir Andrew, write a letter to your parents explaining why you have given up your pursuit of Olivia.

2. a) In this scene, Sir Andrew provides an example of another character deceived by words. What characteristics do he and Malvolio share which make them vulnerable to Sir Toby's manipulations? What is different about them? Do you sympathize with either of them? Why? Record your thoughts and feelings in a journal entry.

   b) What would Andrew and Malvolio look like today? Draw a caricature (a picture or description that exaggerates to an extreme a person's physical features) of a modern-day Andrew or Malvolio.

3. Imagine that Sir Andrew is your younger brother. You overhear Toby convince Andrew to challenge Cesario to a duel and you are concerned that Toby is playing your brother for a fool. You decide to confront Toby. With a partner, role-play the conversation. Present your role-play for another pair. Compare your interpretations of Toby's friendship with Andrew.

4. Toby claims that "report of valour" or an act of bravery is the best way for a man to impress a woman. Do you agree? Divide a blank page in half, and write these headings:
   • what a woman looks for in a man
   • what a man looks for in a woman
   Under each heading, list up to five items. Trade lists with a student of the opposite sex. How do the lists compare? You might want to discuss the similarities and differences with the other person.

   Reflect upon your discussion in a journal entry, entitled "The Surest Way to a Woman's or a Man's Heart."

For the next scene . . .

What are the characteristics of a good friend? What might you do for a friend that you would not do for anyone else?

Act 3, Scene 3

In this scene . . .

Sebastian and Antonio arrive in the city where Orsino holds his court. Because he is wanted in Illyria, Antonio is afraid of being seen and rejects Sebastian's suggestion that they tour the historical sights and monuments of the city. He does not want, however, to spoil Sebastian's fun and gives him money in case Sebastian should want to buy a souvenir. Meanwhile, Antonio intends to go directly to the Elephant inn to make arrangements for their food and lodging.

1   *by my will:* willingly

2   *you make . . . pains:* You take pleasure in your trouble.

3   *chide:* scold

5   *filed:* sharpened; *spur:* urge, incite

6   *not all love:* it was not only love

8   *jealousy:* anxiety

9   *skilless in:* unfamiliar with

12   *The rather . . . fear:* reinforced by these concerns for your safety

16   *shuffled off:* disregarded; *uncurrent pay:* worthless thanks

17   *worth:* resources, wealth; *conscience:* sense of obligation

18   *dealing:* treatment

19   *reliques:* antiquities, ancient sights

21   *'tis long to night:* There is a long time before nightfall.

24   *renown:* make famous; *Would you'd pardon me:* I hope that you will excuse me.

26   *the count his galleys:* the Count's galleys

28   *ta'en:* taken, arrested; *scarce be answer'd:* I would have a difficult time defending myself in a court of law.

29   *Belike:* likely, probably

Scene 3

A street.

Enter Sebastian and Antonio.

Sebastian: I would not by my will have troubled you;
  But, since you make your pleasure of your pains,
  I will no further chide you.
Antonio: I could not stay behind you. My desire,
  More sharp than filed steel, did spur me forth;
  And not all love to see you, though so much
  As might have drawn one to a longer voyage,
  But jealousy what might befall your travel,
  Being skilless in these parts, which to a stranger,
  Unguided and unfriended, often prove
  Rough and unhospitable. My willing love,   10
  The rather by these arguments of fear,
  Set forth in your pursuit.
Sebastian: My kind Antonio,
  I can no other answer make but thanks,
  And thanks, and ever thanks. Often good turns   15
  Are shuffled off with such uncurrent pay;
  But, were my worth as is my conscience firm,
  You should find better dealing. What's to do?
  Shall we go see the reliques of this town?
Antonio: To-morrow, sir. Best first go see your lodging. 20
Sebastian: I am not weary, and 'tis long to night.
  I pray you, let us satisfy our eyes
  With the memorials and the things of fame
  That do renown this city.
Antonio: Would you'd pardon me;
  I do not without danger walk these streets.
  Once, in a sea-fight, 'gainst the count his galleys 25
  I did some service; of such note indeed,
  That were I ta'en here it would scarce be answer'd.
Sebastian: Belike you slew great number of his people.

31   *Albeit the . . . quarrel:* although the circumstances of the occasion and the disagreement

32   *bloody argument:* reason for bloodshed

33-35   *It might . . . did:* Since that time, we could have settled the matter by repaying what we had taken. Most of us did this so that we could continue our trading with the city.

35   *stood out:* held out

36   *lapsed:* arrested

37   *open:* openly

38   *It doth not fit me:* It would not be wise for me.

39   *Elephant:* the name of an inn

40   *bespeak our diet:* order our meals

41   *beguile the time:* amuse yourself

42   *have me:* find me

44   *Haply:* perhaps; *toy:* trifle

45-46   *your store,/ . . . markets:* You do not have enough money to make unnecessary purchases.

47   *I'll be your purse-bearer:* I'll carry your purse.

Antonio: The offence is not of such a bloody nature; 30
Albeit the quality of the time and quarrel
Might well have given us bloody argument.
It might have since been answer'd in repaying
What we took from them, which, for traffic's sake,
Most of our city did. Only myself stood out; 35
For which, if I be lapsed in this place,
I shall pay dear.
Sebastian: Do not then walk too open.
Antonio: It doth not fit me. Hold, sir, here's my purse.
In the south suburbs, at the Elephant,
Is best to lodge. I will bespeak our diet, 40
Whiles you beguile the time and feed your knowledge
With viewing of the town. There shall you have me.
Sebastian: Why I your purse?
Antonio: Haply your eye shall light upon some toy
You have desire to purchase; and your store, 45
I think, is not for idle markets, sir.
Sebastian: I'll be your purse-bearer and leave you
For an hour.
Antonio: To the Elephant.
Sebastian: I do remember.   [*Exeunt.*]

Act 3, Scene 3: Activities

1. Create a travel brochure advertising Illyria, including a map of the town as you imagine it. You should mention or illustrate the seashore, the palaces of Orsino, Olivia's home, the town square, the Elephant inn, and some "points of interest" that you think Sebastian might want to visit.

2. As a journalist, create a report on the incident that makes Antonio an enemy of Orsino. Give detailed information on what Antonio did and include comments from the Duke. Your report might take the form of a newspaper article, or you could present or record it as a radio or television broadcast.

3. Sebastian and Viola are now in the same city and are dressed in the same way. Remembering that they are identical twins, predict the events which might happen and their consequences. Compare your list of events with that of a partner.

For the next scene . . .

Recall a time when you (or someone you know) were sure you were right even though others thought you were wrong. How did other people treat you? How did you respond? In the end, who was right? How did you feel?

Act 3, Scene 4

In this scene . . .

Olivia is waiting for Cesario in her garden when Maria
tells her about Malvolio's strange dress and behaviour.
He then appears in yellow, cross-gartered stockings
with a broad grin on his face. His conversation with
Olivia strikes her as most bizarre, and she becomes
quite worried about his mental health. Olivia places
Malvolio in the care and keeping of Sir Toby, who
immediately furthers the scheme of revenge against
Malvolio by locking him in a dark room.

Sir Andrew enters with the challenge he has written to
Cesario. Toby sends him to wait in a corner of the
garden, deciding to issue the challenge to Cesario by
word of mouth. The challenge terrifies Viola, and only
with difficulty do Toby and Fabian bring her and Andrew
together for a duel. Just as it is about to begin,
Antonio enters. Mistaking Cesario/Viola for Sebastian,
he quickly offers to fight on Sebastian's behalf. When
Toby draws his sword to fight the meddling Antonio,
the Duke's officers enter and arrest Antonio. Still
thinking Cesario/Viola to be Sebastian, Antonio asks for
the return of his purse. When Viola replies that she
has no purse, Antonio is completely bewildered. He
cannot understand why the young gentleman to
whom he has been so kind would abandon him in his
hour of need.

2   *of:* on

3   *youth:* young people

5   *sad and civil:* serious and formal

6   *fortunes:* hard times

9   *possessed:* mad (i.e., possessed by a devil)

13   *tainted in's wits:* out of his mind

15   *merry madness:* that is, love

19   *upon a sad occasion:* about a serious matter

23   *sonnet:* song

23-24   *"Please one, and please/all":* As long as I please the one I love, I really do not care about any others.

25   *how dost thou:* How are you?

27   *black:* sad; *yellow in my legs:* Malvolio's yellow stockings. (Yellow was associated with melancholy during the Renaissance.)

28   *It:* that is, the letter; *his hands:* the hands of the man you intended

29   *sweet Roman hand:* fashionable Italian style of writing, more elegant than traditional English script

Scene 4

Olivia's garden.

Enter Olivia and Maria.

Olivia: I have sent after him; he says he'll come.
How shall I feast him? what bestow of him?
For youth is bought more oft than begg'd or borrow'd.
I speak too loud.
Where is Malvolio? He is sad and civil,
And suits well for a servant with my fortunes:
Where is Malvolio?

Maria: He's coming, madam; but in very strange manner.
He is, sure, possessed, madam.

Olivia: Why, what's the matter? Does he rave?   10

Maria: No, madam, he does nothing but smile. Your ladyship were best to have some guard about you, if he
come; for, sure, the man is tainted in's wits.

Olivia: Go call him hither. [*Exit Maria.*] I am as mad
as he,
If sad and merry madness equal be.   15
[*Re-enter Maria, with Malvolio.*] How now, Malvolio!

Malvolio: Sweet lady, ho, ho.

Olivia: Smilest thou?
I sent for thee upon a sad occasion.

Malvolio: Sad, lady! I could be sad. This does make some   20
obstruction in the blood, this cross-gartering; but
what of that? If it please the eye of one, it is with me
as the very true sonnet is, "Please one, and please
all".

Olivia: Why, how dost thou, man? What is the matter with   25
thee?

Malvolio: Not black in my mind, though yellow in my legs.
It did come to his hands, and commands shall be
executed. I think we do know the sweet Roman hand.

Olivia: Wilt thou go to bed, Malvolio?   30

35   *At your request:* Malvolio will not answer Maria, his social inferior, unless Olivia asks him to; *Yes, nightingales answer daws:* I will answer her, for sometimes fine fellows like me (*nightingales*) do condescend to speak to lowly creatures (*daws*) like Maria.

45   *restore thee:* i.e., to your wits

51   *made:* In Shakespeare's time, *made* and *mad* were pronounced the same way. Olivia, who does not know about the letter, thinks that Malvolio is saying that *she* is mad.

54   *midsummer madness:* extreme folly. It was believed that the full moon of Midsummer's Eve (June 23) could jumble a person's wits and cause eccentric behaviour.

56   *I could . . . back:* I had great difficulty holding him back.

57   *attends your ladyship's pleasure:* waits to hear what you wish of him

59   *looked to:* looked after, cared for

61   *miscarry:* come to any harm

62   *come near me:* understand my importance

63   *concurs:* agrees

65   *stubborn:* rude, hostile

Malvolio: To bed? *Ay, sweetheart, and I'll come to thee.*
Olivia: God comfort thee! Why dost thou smile so and kiss
    thy hand so oft?
Maria: How do you, Malvolio?
Malvolio: At your request! Yes, nightingales answer daws. 35
Maria: Why appear you with this ridiculous boldness be-
    fore my lady?
Malvolio: "Be not afraid of greatness." 'Twas well writ.
Olivia: What meanest thou by that, Malvolio?
Malvolio: "Some are born great,"— 40
Olivia: Ha!
Malvolio: "Some achieve greatness,"—
Olivia: What sayest thou?
Malvolio: "And some have greatness thrust upon them."
Olivia: Heaven restore thee! 45
Malvolio: "Remember who commended thy yellow
    stockings,"—
Olivia: Thy yellow stockings!
Malvolio: "And wished to see thee cross-gartered."
Olivia: Cross-gartered! 50
Malvolio: "Go to, thou art made, if thou desirest to be so;"—
Olivia: Am I made?
Malvolio: "If not, let me see thee a servant still."
Olivia: Why, this is very midsummer madness.
    [*Enter Servant.*]
Servant: Madam, the young gentleman of the Count 55
    Orsino's is returned. I could hardly entreat him back.
    He attends your ladyship's pleasure.
Olivia: I'll come to him. [*Exit Servant.*] Good Maria, let
    this fellow be looked to. Where's my cousin Toby? Let
    some of my people have a special care of him. I would 60
    not have him miscarry for the half of my dowry.
                    [*Exeunt Olivia and Maria.*]
Malvolio: Oho! Do you come near me now? No worse man
    than Sir Toby to look to me! This concurs directly
    with the letter: she sends him on purpose, that I may
    appear stubborn to him; for she incites me to that 65
    in the letter. "Cast thy humble slough," says she; "be
    opposite with a kinsman, surly with servants; let thy
    tongue tang with arguments of state; put thyself into the

69   *consequently:* then, next

69-70   *sets down the/manner how:* describes the way I should do it

70   *sad:* serious; *reverend carriage:* dignified bearing or posture

71   *in the habit of some sir of note:* wearing clothing that would suit an important gentleman

72   *limed:* caught. Birds were caught with birdlime, a sticky substance.

74   *fellow:* Originally, this word meant companion. Later, it came to mean a menial servant. Malvolio chooses to believe that Olivia has used the word in its original meaning (line 53).

75   *after my degree:* according to my position (as a servant in Olivia's household)

76   *no dram of a scruple:* not a small bit (of doubt). A *dram* is one-eighth of a fluid ounce.

76-77   *no scru-/ple of a scruple:* not the smallest bit (of doubt). Malvolio puns on *scruple,* one-third of a dram.

77   *incredulous:* incredible; *unsafe:* uncertain

79   *full prospect:* complete fulfilment

80   *Jove:* another name for Jupiter

82   *sanctity:* holiness

83   *be drawn in little:* gathered into a small place (i.e., Malvolio's body); *Legion:* another name for the Devil (Mark 5:9)

87   *I discard you:* I want nothing to do with you; *private:* privacy

89   *hollow:* deeply

94   *Let me alone:* Let me handle him myself.

95   *Defy:* renounce

98   *La you:* look you

98-99   *takes/it at heart:* is upset, distressed

100   *water:* urine (for medical analysis); *wise woman:* a woman who could cure illnesses and undo witchcraft by means of charms and herbal remedies

101-102 *if I/live:* as surely as I'm alive

107   *move:* anger

trick of singularity;" and consequently sets down the
manner how: as, a sad face, a reverend carriage, a   70
slow tongue, in the habit of some sir of note, and so
forth. I have limed her; but it is Jove's doing, and
Jove make me thankful! And when she went away now,
"Let this fellow be looked to". "Fellow!" not Malvolio, nor after my degree, but "fellow". Why, everything   75
adheres together, that no dram of a scruple, no scruple of a scruple, no obstacle, no incredulous or unsafe
circumstance—What can be said? Nothing that can
be can come between me and the full prospect of my
hopes. Well, Jove, not I, is the doer of this, and he   80
is to be thanked.

[*Re-enter Maria, with Sir Toby and Fabian.*]

Sir Toby: Which way is he, in the name of sanctity? If all
the devils of hell be drawn in little, and Legion
himself possessed him, yet I'll speak to him.

Fabian: Here he is, here he is. How is't with you, sir? How   85
is't with you, man?

Malvolio: Go off; I discard you. Let me enjoy my private.
Go off.

Maria: Lo, how hollow the fiend speaks within him! Did
not I tell you? Sir Toby, my lady prays you to have a   90
care of him.

Malvolio: Aha! does she so?

Sir Toby: Go to, go to; peace, peace; we must deal gently
with him. Let me alone. How do you, Malvolio? how
is't with you? What, man! Defy the devil. Consider,   95
he's an enemy to mankind.

Malvolio: Do you know what you say?

Maria: La you, an you speak ill of the devil, how he takes
it at heart! Pray God, he be not bewitched!

Fabian: Carry his water to th' wise woman.   100

Maria: Marry, and it shall be done tomorrow morning, if I
live. My lady would not lose him for more than I'll
say.

Malvolio: How now, mistress!

Maria: O Lord!   105

Sir Toby: Prithee, hold thy peace; this is not the way. Do
you not see you move him? let me alone with him.

110   *bawcock:* fine fellow (from the French *beau coq*)

111   *chuck?:* chick (a term of affection)

113   *Biddy:* chicken. (Another term of endearment, usually used with young children.)

114   *for gravity:* suitable for a person of dignity; *cherry-pit:* a children's game in which cherry pits were thrown into numbered holes

115   *foul collier:* dirty coalman. Coalmen were associated with the devil because they were covered with black soot.

118   *minx:* hussy, shameless woman.

121   *I am not of your element:* I do not belong to your world.

121-122   *You shall know more/hereafter:* You will hear more about this later.

126   *genius:* soul, spirit; *taken:* caught (as one catches a disease)

127   *device:* scheme

128-129   *take air and/taint:* be exposed to air (i.e, be discovered) and turn sour

132   *in a dark room and bound:* This was the usual treatment for madness.

134   *carry:* continue (both with our joke and with the belief that he is mad); *penance:* suffering

135   *pastime:* entertainment

136-137   *bring the/ . . . bar:* reveal our trick to everyone. (The metaphor here is legal, the *bar* being the place in court where the prisoner stands.)

137   *crown:* appoint

137-138   *finder of madmen:* one who decides whether or not a person will be declared insane

139   *More matter for a May morning:* another subject for holiday fun. The month of May was traditionally associated with games and celebration.

142   *saucy:* spicy (as a metaphor for *insolent* and *rude*), picking up on *vinegar* and *pepper* (line 141)

145   *scurvy:* contemptible

Fabian: No way but gentleness; gently, gently. The fiend
    is rough, and will not be roughly used.

Sir Toby: Why, how now, my bawcock! How dost thou,   110
    chuck?

Malvolio: Sir!

Sir Toby: Ay, Biddy, come with me. What, man! 'Tis not
    for gravity to play at cherry-pit with Satan. Hang
    him, foul collier!   115

Maria: Get him to say his prayers, good Sir Toby, get him
    to pray.

Malvolio: My prayers, minx!

Maria: No, I warrant you, he will not hear of godliness.

Malvolio: Go, hang yourselves all! You are idle shallow   120
    things; I am not of your element. You shall know more
    hereafter.   [*Exit.*]

Sir Toby: Is't possible?

Fabian: If this were played upon a stage now, I could
    condemn it as an improbable fiction.   125

Sir Toby: His very genius hath taken the infection of the
    device, man.

Maria: Nay, pursue him now, lest the device take air and
    taint.

Fabian: Why, we shall make him mad indeed.   130

Maria: The house will be the quieter.

Sir Toby: Come, we'll have him in a dark room and bound.
    My niece is already in the belief that he's mad. We
    may carry it thus, for our pleasure and his penance,
    till our very pastime, tired out of breath, prompt us to   135
    have mercy on him, at which time we will bring the
    device to the bar and crown thee for a finder of mad-
    men. But see, but see!
    [*Enter Sir Andrew.*]

Fabian: More matter for a May morning.

Sir Andrew: Here's the challenge, read it. I warrant there's   140
    vinegar and pepper in't.

Fabian: Is't so saucy?

Sir Andrew: Ay, is't, I warrant him. Do but read.

Sir Toby: Give me. [*Reads.*] *Youth, whatsoever thou art, thou
    art but a scurvy fellow.*   145

Fabian: Good, and valiant.

147 *admire:* marvel

149-150 *A good . . . law:* Sir Andrew will not be liable to legal action (*blow of the/law*) because he has not made any specific accusations against Viola/Cesario.

152 *uses:* treats

155 *waylay:* ambush

159 *o' the windy side:* on the safe side

161-162 *my hope/is better:* I hope for a better, that is, happier result.

165 *very fit occasion:* an excellent opportunity

166 *commerce:* conversation

168 *scout me:* I suggest that you keep watch.

169 *bum-baily:* bailiff, an officer employed by a sheriff to make arrests. (Toby's slang suggests that bailiffs are cowards who sneak up on people from behind.)

172 *sharply twanged off:* fiercely pronounced

173 *approbation:* reputation (for courage); *proof:* an actual deed (of courage)

175 *let me alone for swearing:* No one can swear as well as I.

177-178 *of good/capacity and breeding:* intelligent and well-educated

180 *breed:* cause, bring about

181 *clodpole:* dunce, blockhead

182-183 *set/upon . . . valour:* report Aguecheek to be a man of remarkable courage

183 *drive:* lead

184 *aptly receive:* quickly believe

185 *hideous:* fearful

Sir Toby: [*Reads.*] *Wonder not, nor admire not in thy mind,*
   why I do call thee so, for I will show thee no reason for't.
Fabian: A good note; that keeps you from the blow of the
   law.   150
Sir Toby: [*Reads.*] *Thou comest to the lady Olivia, and in my*
   sight she uses thee kindly; but thou liest in thy throat.
   That is not the matter I challenge thee for.
Fabian: Very brief, and to exceeding good sense—less.
Sir Toby: [*Reads.*] *I will waylay thee going home, where if it*   155
   be thy chance to kill me—
Fabian: Good.
Sir Toby: [*Reads.*] *Thou killest me like a rogue and a villain.*
Fabian: Still you keep o' the windy side of the law; good.
Sir Toby: [*Reads.*] *Fare thee well; and God have mercy upon one*   160
   of our souls! He may have mercy upon mine; but my hope
   is better, and so look to thyself. Thy friend, as thou usest
   him, and thy sworn enemy, Andrew Aguecheek. If this
   letter move him not, his legs cannot. I'll give it him.
Maria: You may have very fit occasion for't; he is now in   165
   some commerce with my lady, and will by and by
   depart.
Sir Toby: Go, Sir Andrew; scout me for him at the corner
   of the orchard like a bum-baily. So soon as ever thou
   seest him, draw; and, as thou drawest, swear horrible;   170
   for it comes to pass oft that a terrible oath, with a
   swaggering accent sharply twanged off, gives
   manhood more approbation than ever proof itself would
   have earned him. Away!
Sir Andrew: Nay, let me alone for swearing.   [*Exit.*]   175
Sir Toby: Now will not I deliver his letter: for the behaviour
   of the young gentleman gives him out to be of good
   capacity and breeding; his employment between his lord
   and my niece confirms no less. Therefore this letter,
   being so excellently ignorant, will breed no terror in the   180
   youth. He will find it comes from a clodpole. But, sir,
   I will deliver his challenge by word of mouth; set
   upon Aguecheek a notable report of valour; and drive
   the gentleman, as I know his youth will aptly receive
   it, into a most hideous opinion of his rage, skill, fury   185

[Handwritten note in margin: Don't be scared of the letter.]

167

187   *cockatrices:* imaginary reptiles, considered to be the most deadly of all creatures, able to kill with a single glance

188   *give them way:* Keep out of their way.

189   *presently after him:* immediately follow him

190   *the while:* meanwhile; *horrid:* frightening, horrifying

193   *laid:* risked; *unchary:* carelessly

194   *reproves:* scolds

197   *'haviour:* behaviour

199   *jewel:* probably a locket containing a portrait of Olivia

200   *vex:* annoy

202-203 *What shall . . . give?:* I'll give you whatever you ask as long as I can do so without any risk to my sense of honour. Olivia's question is rhetorical; it makes a statement of her generous love.

206   *acquit you:* relieve you of your promise (as a judge or jury *acquits* a person from a criminal charge)

210   *That defence . . . to't:* Whatever means of protection you have, use them.

212   *intercepter:* attacker; *despite:* defiance

212-213 *bloody as the/hunter:* bloodthirsty as a hunting dog

213   *attends thee:* waits for you

213-214 *Dismount/thy tuck:* Unsheathe or take out your rapier.

214   *yare:* quick, nimble

217   *to:* with; *remembrance:* memory

218   *image:* recollection

220   *if you . . . price:* if you consider your life to be worth anything

221   *opposite:* opponent

222   *furnish man withal:* equip a man with

[handwritten: imaginary reptile]

and impetuosity. This will so fright them both that they
will kill one another by the look, like cockatrices.
[*Re-enter Olivia, with Viola.*]
Fabian: Here he comes with your niece; give them way till *[handwritten: wait till they leave so we can talk]*
he take leave, and presently after him.
Sir Toby: I will meditate the while upon some horrid message 190
for a challenge. [*Exeunt Sir Toby, Fabian, and Maria.*]
Olivia: I have said too much unto a heart of stone *[handwritten: she told him everything, ladies aren't to do that. Bad girl.]*
And laid mine honour too unchary out.
There's something in me that reproves my fault;
But such a headstrong potent fault it is,
That it but mocks reproof.
Viola: With the same 'haviour that your passion bears *[handwritten: it has my]*
Goes on my master's grief. *[handwritten: what is this locket, picture in it?]*
Olivia: Here, wear this jewel for me, 'tis my picture.
Refuse it not; it hath no tongue to vex you;   200
And I beseech you come again to-morrow.
What shall you ask of me that I'll deny,
That honour saved may upon asking give?
Viola: Nothing but this, your true love for my master.
Olivia: How with mine honour may I give him that   205
Which I have given to you?
Viola: I will acquit you.
Olivia: Well, come again to-morrow. Fare thee well. [*Exit.*]
[*Re-enter Sir Toby and Fabian.*]
Sir Toby: Gentleman, God save thee.
Viola: And you, sir.
Sir Toby: That defence thou hast, betake thee to't. Of what 210
nature the wrongs are thou hast done him, I know
not; but thy intercepter, full of despite, bloody as the *[handwritten: whatever you did Sir Andrew is mad and you better meet him at the orchard.]*
hunter, attends thee at the orchard-end. Dismount
thy tuck, be yare in thy preparation, for thy assailant
is quick, skilful, and deadly.   215
Viola: You mistake, sir; I am sure no man hath any quarrel
to me. My remembrance is very free and clear from
any image of offence done to any man.
Sir Toby: You'll find it otherwise, I assure you. Therefore,
if you hold your life at any price, betake you to your   220
guard; for your opposite hath in him what youth,
strength, skill, and wrath can furnish man withal.

224	*dubbed with unhatched rapier:* He was made a knight without having used his sword in battle.
225	*on carpet consideration:* on the basis of his connections at court
226	*Souls and bodies . . . three:* He has killed three men.
227	*incensement:* anger
228	*satisfaction can be none but:* he will only be satisfied
229	*sepulchre:* burial. (A sepulchre is a tomb); *Hob, nob:* have it, or have it not; *give't or take't:* kill, or be killed. (The *it* is death.)
230-231	*desire some/conduct:* ask for an escort
233	*taste:* test; *Belike:* perhaps
234	*quirk:* peculiar habit or "twist" of behaviour
235	*derives itself out of:* is caused by
235-236	*very/competent:* sufficient
237	*Back you shall not:* You will not return.
238	*that:* i.e., a fight
239	*answer:* satisfy
239-240	*strip your/sword stark naked:* Draw your sword (and fight with me).
240	*meddle:* engage, fight
241	*forswear to . . . you:* give up your right to wear a sword (by proving that you are a coward)
243	*know of the knight:* find out from the knight
244-245	*It is something . . . purpose:* It must be something I did by accident.
250	*mortal arbitrement:* fight to the death
253-254	*to read him/by his form:* to judge him by his appearance
254-255	*in the proof/of his valour:* when you put his courage to the test
256	*fatal:* deadly; *opposite:* opponent
259	*bound:* obliged, indebted
260	*sir priest:* Priests were called *sir* out of respect.
261	*mettle:* generally, character; here probably, courage

Who is this guy.

Viola: I pray you, sir, what is he?

Sir Toby: He is knight, dubbed with unhatched rapier and on carpet consideration; but he is a devil in private brawl. Souls and bodies hath he divorced three; and his incensement at this moment is so implacable, that satisfaction can be none but by pangs of death and sepulchre. Hob, nob, is his word; give't or take't.

Viola: I will return again into the house and desire some   230
conduct of the lady. I am no fighter. I have heard of some kind of men that put quarrels purposely on others, to taste their valour. Belike this is a man of that quirk.

Sir Toby: Sir, no; his indignation derives itself out of a very   235
competent injury. Therefore, get you on and give him his desire. Back you shall not to the house, unless you undertake that with me which with as much safety you might answer him. Therefore, on, or strip your sword stark naked; for meddle you must, that's certain,   240
or forswear to wear iron about you.

Viola: This is as uncivil as strange. I beseech you, do me this courteous office, as to know of the knight what my offence to him is. It is something of my negligence, nothing of my purpose.   245

Sir Toby: I will do so. Signior Fabian, stay you by this gentleman till my return.   [*Exit.*]

Viola: Pray you, sir, do you know of this matter?

Fabian: I know the knight is incensed against you, even to a mortal arbitrement; but nothing of the circumstance   250
more.

Viola: I beseech you, what manner of man is he?

Fabian: Nothing of that wonderful promise, to read him by his form, as you are like to find him in the proof of his valour. He is, indeed, sir, the most skilful,   255
bloody, and fatal opposite that you could possibly have found in any part of Illyria. Will you walk towards him? I will make your peace with him if I can.

Viola: I shall be much bound to you for't. I am one that had rather go with sir priest than sir knight. I care not   260
who knows so much of my mettle.   [*Exeunt.*]

225

Never used his riffle, always its court. Sir andrew is a puppy dog at the kings feet. He is the Kings favorite (Carpet knight

Pull your sword out of its core (personification)

Tries to frighten Viola + Sir Andrew.

171

263   *firago:* Toby means *virago*, a warlike woman. (But Toby does not know that Cesario is Viola in disguise); *pass:* duel, fencing match

264   *stuck in:* Toby means *stoccado*, a thrust in fencing.

264-265 *mortal/motion:* deadly action

265   *it is inevitable:* his victory was assured; *on the answer:* in a return hit

267   *Sophy:* the Shah of Persia

271   *Plague on't:* curse it

272   *cunning in fence:* skilful at fencing

273   *Let him . . . slip:* if he is willing to forget the matter

275   *motion:* suggestion

276   *perdition of souls:* loss of lives

279   *take up:* settle

281   *He is as . . . him:* Viola/Cesario is just as afraid of Sir Andrew.

283   *remedy:* escape

284   *for oath's sake:* because he has vowed he will

284-285 *better/bethought him of:* taken another look at, reconsidered

286-287 *for the/supportance of his vow:* so that he may claim to have kept his promise

287   *protests:* promises

289   *A little thing would:* it would not take much to

290   *how much I lack of a man:* that I am not a man

291   *Give ground:* retreat

293   *bout:* Fencing matches are divided into rounds or *bouts*.

294   *duello:* code of duelling

296   *to't:* get to it

Not good with words.

Dramatic Irony

[*Re-enter Sir Toby, with Sir Andrew.*]

Sir Toby: Why, man, he's a very devil; I have not seen such
a firago. I had a pass with him, rapier, scabbard and
all, and he gives me the stuck in with such a mortal
motion, that it is inevitable; and on the answer, he
pays you as surely as your feet hit the ground they step
on. They say he has been fencer to the Sophy.

Mistake virago.

A coward thin & weedy

practice fight

Person who uses the rapier

Sir Andrew: I'll not meddle with him.

Sir Toby: Ay, but he will not now be pacified. Fabian can
scarce hold him yonder.   270

Sir Andrew: Plague on't, an' I thought he had been valiant
and so cunning in fence, I'ld not have challenged
him. Let him let the matter slip, and I'll give him my
horse, grey Capilet.

Sir Toby: I'll make the motion. Stand here, make a good   275
show on't; this shall end without the perdition of souls.
[*Aside.*] Marry, I'll ride your horse as well as I ride
you. *Pun.*

[*Re-enter Fabian and Viola.*]

[*To Fabian.*] I have his horse to take up the quarrel; I
have persuaded him the youth's a devil.   280

Fabian: He is as horribly conceited of him; and pants and
looks pale, as if a bear were at his heels. *Very Scared*

Sir Toby: [*To Viola.*] There's no remedy, sir; he will fight
with you for oath's sake. Marry, he hath better
bethought him of his quarrel, and he finds that now   285
scarce to be worth talking of; therefore draw, for the
supportance of his vow. He protests he will not hurt
you.

Viola: [*Aside.*] Pray God defend me! A little thing would
make me tell them how much I lack of a man. *Dramatic* 290
Irony.

Fabian: Give ground, if you see him furious.

Sir Toby: Come, Sir Andrew, there's no remedy; the
gentleman will, for his honour's sake, have one bout
with you; he cannot by the duello avoid it. But he has
promised me, as he is a gentleman and a soldier, he   295
will not hurt you. Come on; to't.

Sir Andrew: Pray God, he keep his oath!

Viola: I do assure you, 'tis against my will.   [*They draw.*]

301   *I for him defy you:* I challenge you on his behalf.

305   *undertaker:* one who takes up a challenge for another; *I am for you:* I am ready for you.

306   *officers:* Orsino's police

307   *anon:* later

308   *up:* away

309   *that I promised you:* i.e., the horse that Sir Andrew promised in line 283

311   *reins well:* responds well to your use of his reins

312   *office:* duty

313   *at the suit:* on the authority of

316   *no jot:* not a bit; *favour:* face

320   *I shall answer it:* I will have to stand trial for my crime (see Act 3, Scene 3, lines 25-37).

321   *necessity:* need

324   *befalls myself:* is happening to me; *amazed:* in amazement

325   *be of comfort:* Cheer up.

327   *entreat of you:* ask you for

330   *part:* partly

331   *lean and low ability:* very little means

332   *My having is not much:* I do not have much.

333   *I'll make . . . you:* I'll give you half of what money I now have.

334   *coffer:* money (literally, money chest); *deny:* refuse

[Enter Antonio.]

Antonio: Put up your sword. If this young gentleman
    Have done offence, I take the fault on me. *I'll fight*   300
    If you offend him, I for him defy you. *fr you.*

Sir Toby: You sir! why, what are you?

Antonio: One, sir, that for his love dares yet do more
    Than you have heard him brag to you he will.

Sir Toby: Nay, if you be an undertaker, I am for you.   305
             be a ring'y   *[They draw.]*

[Enter Officers.]

Fabian: O good Sir Toby, hold! here come the officers.

Sir Toby: *[To Antonio.]* I'll be with you anon.

Viola: Pray, sir, put your sword up, if you please.

Sir Andrew: Marry, will I, sir; and for that I promised you,
    I'll be as good as my word. He will bear you easily   310
    and reins well.

First Officer: This is the man; do thy office. *Take him away*

Second Officer: Antonio, I arrest thee at the suit of Count
    Orsino.

Antonio: You do mistake me, sir.   315

First Officer: No, sir, no jot; I know your favour well,
    Though now you have no sea-cap on your head. *Coherance*
    Take him away; he knows I know him well.

Antonio: I must obey. *[To Viola.]* This comes with seeking
    you:
    But there's no remedy; I shall answer it.   320
    What will you do, now my necessity   ——— *He needs his*
    Makes me to ask you for my purse? It grieves me *purse to bribe officers.*
    Much more for what I cannot do for you
    Than what befalls myself. You stand amazed;
    But be of comfort.   325

Second Officer: Come, sir, away.

Antonio: I must entreat of you some of that money.

Viola: What money, sir?
    For the fair kindness you have show'd me here,
    And, part, being prompted by your present trouble,   330
    Out of my lean and low ability
    I'll lend you something. My having is not much;
    I'll make division of my present with you.
    Hold, there's half my coffer.

335-336   *my deserts . . . persuasion:* my claims on you can fail to persuade you

336   *tempt:* provoke

337   *unsound:* morally weak. (It would be improper for Antonio to seek repayment for his kindnesses to Sebastian; good deeds should be performed for their own sakes.)

338   *upbraid:* reproach, scold

342   *vainness:* both boasting and falseness

343   *taint:* spot, trace

348   *Relieved him:* looked after him; *sanctity:* purity

349   *image:* what he appeared to be

349-350   *which methought . . . worth:* which looked to me like it deserved to be worshipped

350   *did I devotion:* I gave devotion

352   *vile:* shameful, disgusting

353   *Thou hast . . . shame:* You have shamed physical beauty (*good feature*), by proving that it does not always reflect inner goodness.

355   *unkind:* unnatural

356   *the beauteous-evil:* those who are outwardly beautiful but evil within

357   *trunks:* bodies; *o'erflourish'd:* covered with ornamental paintings and carvings (i.e., made outwardly beautiful)

362   *So do not I:* I do not believe myself (as he does).

364   *ta'en:* taken, mistaken

366   *sage saws:* wise sayings

368   *glass:* mirror. (Because Viola and Sebastian are identical twins, she sees him each time she looks in the mirror.); *even such and so:* just like this

369   *favour:* face

369-370   *went/Still:* always dressed

371   *if it prove:* if it turns out to be true (that Sebastian is alive)

Antonio: Will you deny me now?
Is't possible that my deserts to you   335
Can lack persuasion? Do not tempt my misery,
Lest that it make me so unsound a man
As to upbraid you with those kindnesses
That I have done for you.
Viola: I know of none. *She doesn't*
Nor know I you by voice or any feature. *remember.* 340
I hate ingratitude more in a man
Than lying vainness, babbling drunkenness,
Or any taint of vice whose strong corruption
Inhabits our frail blood.
Antonio: O heavens themselves!
Second Officer: Come, sir, I pray you, go.   345
Antonio: Let me speak a little. This youth that you see here *Antonio*
I snatch'd one half out of the jaws of death, *saved him!*
Relieved him with such sanctity of love,
And to his image, which methought did promise
Most venerable worth, did I devotion.   350
First Officer: What's that to us? The time goes by; away!
Antonio: But oh, how vile an idol proves this god! *you have insulted*
Thou hast, Sebastian, done good feature shame. *yourself.*
In nature there's no blemish but the mind;
None can be called deform'd but the unkind;   355
Virtue is beauty, but the beauteous-evil *oxymoron!*
Are empty trunks o'erflourish'd by the devil.
First Officer: The man grows mad; away with him!
Come, come, sir.
Antonio: Lead me on.   [*Exit with Officers.*] 360
Viola: Methinks his words do from such passion fly,
That he believes himself. So do not I.
Prove true, imagination, O prove true,
That I, dear brother, be now ta'en for you!
Sir Toby: Come hither, knight; come hither, Fabian; we'll 365
whisper o'er a couplet or two of most sage saws.
Viola: He named Sebastian. I my brother know
Yet living in my glass; even such and so
In favour was my brother, and he went
Still in this fashion, colour, ornament,   370
For him I imitate. Oh, if it prove,

373   *dishonest:* dishonourable; *paltry:* worthless, contemptible

374   *dishonesty:* dishonour; *appears:* is revealed by

375   *denying him:* refusing to acknowledge that he knows him

376   *cowardship:* cowardice

377   *devout:* devoted; *religious in it:* completely dedicated to his cowardice

378   *'Slid:* by God's eyelid

379   *cuff him soundly:* slap him hard

381   *event:* outcome

382   *lay:* bet, wager; *yet:* after all

it washes
it Sabatien a shore
(paradox)

in Illyria.
so he likes

Tempests are kind and salt waves fresh in love.   [*Exit.*]
Sir Toby: A very dishonest paltry boy, and more a coward
than a hare. His dishonesty appears in leaving his
friend here in necessity and denying him; and for his   375
cowardship, ask Fabian.
Fabian: A coward, a most devout coward, religious in it.

He's a coward and I am angry

Sir Andrew: 'Slid, I'll after him again and beat him.
Sir Toby: Do; cuff him soundly, but never draw thy sword.
Sir Andrew: An I do not,—   [*Exit.*] 380
Fabian: Come, let's see the event.
Sir Toby: I dare lay any money 'twill be nothing yet.
                                      [*Exeunt.*]

Act 3, Scene 4: Activities

1. Much of the humour in the first half of this scene
   is physical: the comedy depends more upon the
   appearance and actions of the characters than upon
   the words they speak. Because Shakespeare gives
   us few stage directions, we must supply these elements
   from our imagination. Choose either the scene segment in which Malvolio appears cross-gartered before
   Olivia (lines 16–54) or the confrontation between Sir
   Toby and Malvolio (lines 82–138). In a group of three or
   four, read the segment aloud several times, looking
   for places where facial expression, gesture, and movement might help to make the scene funnier.

   Rehearse the lines, incorporating the actions you have
   invented. After sharing your scene segment with
   other groups, discuss the variety of comic effects you
   have explored. Did your understanding of the segment change after seeing the various dramatizations?
   If so, explain how.

2. How does Malvolio's soliloquy (lines 62–81) reveal that
   he deceives himself as much as the others have
   deceived him? Notice how he misinterprets Olivia's
   reactions in order to support his belief in her affection
   for him.

   As Malvolio, write a diary entry of the day's events in
   which you compile further proof of Olivia's love for you. In
   your entry, try to show the self-deception which Shakespeare reveals in the soliloquy.

3. Again in this scene, Viola is forced to deal with society's
   expectations of the role she has assumed. As a "gentleman," she must defend her honour according to an
   unwritten code of male behaviour. What values, attitudes, and actions does this code require? Discuss
   the commandments which would define this code if

it had been written down in Shakespeare's time and then discuss the following:

a) What similar codes are there today for males? for females? What commandments might define these contemporary codes?

b) Do you find modern codes fair, appropriate, and useful? If not, compose a third list of the commandments which you would support.

4. a) When someone whom we have admired and respected turns out to be unworthy of our admiration and respect, we are likely to experience a very unpleasant emotional letdown. In a journal entry, record an experience in which you or someone you know felt this sense of letdown. Identify the different emotions you felt during this experience.

b) Using the insights you gained from the experience, compose the journal entry which Antonio might have written after his denial and rejection by the man he thought to be Sebastian.

Act 3: Consider the Whole Act

1. In Activity 2 for Act 1, Scene 2, you began a list of words and phrases to describe Viola's personality. Review and revise your list as you consider the three scenes in which Viola appears in this act: her conversation with Feste, her second meeting with Olivia, and her "duel" with Sir Andrew.

Note any changes in her character and personality and new revelations about her for which you were not prepared.

2. Shakespeare uses both poetry and prose in his scripting of the play. Consider, as examples, the dialogue between Viola and Olivia at the end of Scene 1 (lines 145–164) and Sir Toby's speech in Scene 4 (lines 168- 174). Compare the two passages, using the following questions as a guide:
   • What are the subjects discussed?
   • How serious or light are the scenes in which these lines occur?
   • What are the audience's attitudes to the characters in each scene?
   • How does Shakespeare's choice of words and images reinforce the differences in language you have already noticed?
   Share your observations with a partner. Together, try to reach some general conclusions about Shakespeare's use of poetry and prose.

3. "This fellow is wise enough to play the fool;
   And to do that well craves a kind of wit."
   (Scene 1, lines 61–62)
   Review carefully Viola's speech from which these lines are taken. What is she saying about the skill of the "wise fool"?

   a) Document Feste's skill as a wise fool, referring to his fooling with Olivia (Act 1, Scene 5), with Orsino (Act 2, Scene 4), and with Viola (Act 3, Scene 1). Note how his fooling is specifically directed to the individuals with whom he is speaking.

   b) As a class, consider who are some "wise fools" in today's society. How do they draw attention to our follies and weaknesses?

4. Imagine that *Twelfth Night* were a tragedy instead of a comedy. Compose a brief plot synopsis in which you reveal how the final two acts of the play will lead to a tragic ending. Share your ideas in a small group. Select the most promising plot possibilities and script or improvise a final tragic scene for the play.

5. "For folly that he wisely shows is fit;
   But wise men, folly-fall'n, quite taint their wit."
   (Scene 1, lines 68–69)
   The news is full of events which demonstrate the truth
   of this observation about human nature. Use a recent
   news story as the basis for a fable in which Viola's
   comment is the moral.

   As an alternative, create your own news story and report
   it as an on-the-scene journalist.

6. Write a newspaper column in which you summarize the
   social events in Illyria during the past week. Include
   a fashion comment.

7. As an independent or group project, find out all you can
   about the sport of fencing: the rules, the movements,
   the equipment, the scoring, and the terminology. Compare how the sport is played today to how it was
   played in Shakespeare's time.

   As a related project, you might want to research the
   history of challenges and duels as a means of pro-
   tecting one's honour and reputation.

For the next scene . . .

Why might it be unwise to act upon the advice of a friend
without knowing the whole story yourself? How has this
kind of error led you or someone you know into trouble or
danger?

Act 4, Scene 1

In this scene . . .

Feste has been sent by Olivia to find Cesario, but he meets Sebastian first. He thinks Sebastian is Cesario because they look the same. This is only the first of many such mistakes in this scene. Sebastian doesn't know what Feste is talking about and refuses to meet with Olivia. At this moment, Sir Andrew enters and strikes Sebastian a blow to the head. When Sir Toby intervenes to prevent Andrew from being seriously hurt, Sebastian, who Andrew supposes to be the cowardly Cesario, strikes him back. Sir Toby draws his sword on Sebastian just as Olivia appears. She, too, thinks Sebastian is Cesario. She dismisses Sir Toby for his uncivilized behaviour, and invites Sebastian back to her house. Sebastian is completely confused, but he accepts the offer of the beautiful countess.

1 *am not sent:* have not been sent

3 *Go to:* Go away.

4 *clear:* rid

5 *held out:* kept up (his pretending not to recognize Feste)

10 *vent thy folly:* play your silly games

12 *of:* from

13-15 *I/am afraid . . . cockney:* Essentially, Feste is saying that he is so surprised that he will believe anything.

14 *lubber:* lout, "jerk"

15 *cockney:* effeminate or foppish fellow; *ungird thy strangeness:* stop pretending to be a stranger

16 *vent:* say

18 *foolish Greek:* silly clown, merry-maker. In Roman drama, all comic characters were Greek.

19 *tarry:* delay, wait

21 *thou hast an open hand:* You are very generous.

22-23 *re-/port:* reputation

23 *after fourteen years' purchase:* at a high price. (Land was commonly sold at the value of twelve years' rental. Feste adds two more years for emphasis.)

25 *There's for you:* Take that.

28 *Hold:* stop

30 *straight:* at once, immediately

30-31 *in/some of your coats:* in your situation. (Compare the modern expression "in your shoes.")

Act 4, Scene 1

The street before Olivia's house.

Enter Sebastian and Feste.

Feste: Will you make me believe that I am not sent for
  you? ~coherence~
Sebastian: Go to, go to, thou art a foolish fellow.
  Let me be clear of thee. ~go away~
Feste: Well held out, i' faith! No, I do not know you;   5
  nor I am not sent to you by my lady, to bid you
  come speak with her; nor your name is not Master
  Cesario; nor this is not my nose neither. Nothing
  that is so is so. ~What you see is not really / what you get.~
Sebastian: I prithee, vent thy folly somewhere else. Thou   10
  know'st not me.
Feste: Vent my folly! He has heard that word of some great
  man, and now applies it to a fool. Vent my folly! I
  am afraid this great lubber, the world, will prove a
  cockney. I prithee now, ungird thy strangeness and   15
  tell me what I shall vent to my lady. Shall I vent to her
  that thou art coming? ~Classical Allusion.~
Sebastian: I prithee, foolish Greek, depart from me. There's ~Jokes are / comedians.~
  money for thee; if you tarry longer, I shall give worse
  payment.   20
Feste: By my troth, thou hast an open hand. These wise
  men that give fools money get themselves a good report—after fourteen years' purchase.
  [*Enter Sir Andrew, Sir Toby, and Fabian.*]
Sir Andrew: Now, sir, have I met you again? There's for
  you. ~Striking him without a stop rd.~ [*Striking Sebastian.*]   25
Sebastian: Why, there's for thee, and there, and there. Are
  all the people mad? ~Situation / Irony~ [*Beating Sir Andrew.*]
Sir Toby: Hold, sir, or I'll throw your dagger o'er the
  house.
Feste: This will I tell my lady straight; I would not be in   30
  some of your coats for two pence.   [*Exit.*]

33 *work:* fight, contend

34 *action of battery:* charge of assault

39 *iron:* sword; *You are well fleshed:* You have drawn enough blood already.

42 *tempt:* provoke

45 *malapert:* impudent, saucy

46 *charge:* command

48 *Will it be ever thus?:* Is this the way it is always going to be?

50 *preach'd:* taught

52 *Rudesby:* ruffian

53 *sway:* rule

54 *uncivil:* uncivilized, barbarous; *extent:* attack

56 *fruitless:* pointless

57 *botch'd up:* clumsily contrived, patched together

58 *Thou shalt . . . go:* You have no choice but to come with me.

59 *deny:* refuse; *Beshrew:* curse on

60 *started:* startled, alarmed, roused

61 *What relish is in this?:* What am I tasting? (i.e., what does this mean?); *How runs the stream?:* What is happening here?

62 *Or . . . or:* either . . . or

63 *fancy:* imagination; *still:* always; *sense:* reason; *in Lethe steep:* drown in Lethe, the mythological river of forgetfulness in the underworld

64 *would thou'dst be:* I want you to be

66 *say so, and so be:* i.e., say you will be ruled by me, and that is what will happen

Sir Toby: Come on, sir; hold.

Sir Andrew: Nay, let him alone. I'll go another way to work
    with him: I'll have an action of battery against him,
    if there be any law in Illyria; though I struck him first,   35
    yet it's no matter for that.

Sebastian: Let go thy hand.

Sir Toby: Come, sir, I will not let you go. Come, my young
    soldier, put up your iron. You are well fleshed; come
    on.   40

Sebastian: I will be free from thee. What wouldst thou
    now? If thou darest tempt me further, draw thy
    sword.

Sir Toby: What, what? Nay, then I must have an ounce or
    two of this malapert blood from you.   45

    [*Enter Olivia.*]

Olivia: Hold, Toby; on thy life I charge thee, hold!

Sir Toby: Madam!

Olivia: Will it be ever thus? Ungracious wretch,
    Fit for the mountains and the barbarous caves,
    Where manners ne'er were preach'd! Out of my sight!   50
    Be not offended, dear Cesario.
    Rudesby, be gone!

      [*Exeunt Sir Toby, Sir Andrew, and Fabian.*]
      I prithee, gentle friend,
    Let thy fair wisdom, not thy passion, sway
    In this uncivil and unjust extent
    Against thy peace. Go with me to my house,   55
    And hear thou there how many fruitless pranks
    This ruffian hath botch'd up, that thou thereby
    Mayst smile at this. Thou shalt not choose but go.
    Do not deny. Beshrew his soul for me,
    He started one poor heart of mine in thee.   60

Sebastian: What relish is in this? How runs the stream?
    Or I am mad, or else this is a dream.
    Let fancy still my sense in Lethe steep;
    If it be thus to dream, still let me sleep!

Olivia: Nay, come, I prithee; would thou'dst be ruled by
    me!   65

Sebastian: Madam, I will.

Olivia: Oh, say so, and so be!   [*Exeunt.*]

Act 4, Scene 1: Activities

1. Reread this short scene and consider the actions of Sebastian with Feste, then Andrew, and finally Olivia. How does each character confuse Sebastian? What would he tell Antonio about his first experiences in Illyria? With a partner, role-play the conversation they might have.

2. A scene as full of physical action as this one must be choreographed like a dance in order to be successful on stage. In a group of five divide the scene into sections and create a series of diagrams to plot the movements of each of the actors in each section, including entrances and exits. Make sure that you account for everybody on stage, including those who are not speaking. Practise the scene as a pantomime, expressing the actions and emotions through movement only.

   Consider the following questions as you practise:
   • What parts of the scene are easiest to play?
   • What are the most difficult parts? How do you solve the problems?
   • What importance do gestures play in communicating some of the challenging interactions?
   • What stage movements are essential to understanding the language and meaning of the scene?

   Perform the scene for another group, and discuss your performance with them. Was there anything you *couldn't* communicate through action?

3. Create a poster to advertise *Twelfth Night*. Use a moment from this scene as the poster's illustration. Your poster might also feature other information, such as a title, a caption, or a catchy phrase. Present your poster to a small group, explaining why you think it is effective.

For the next scene . . .

At what stage does a practical joke lose its humour? How do you know when to end it?

Act 4, Scene 2

In this scene . . .

Malvolio has been locked in a dark room because he is supposedly insane. Feste disguises himself as a priest (Sir Topas) and visits Malvolio. He pretends to be concerned about Malvolio, but uses the opportunity to mistreat him further. One of the bystanders is Sir Toby, who is amused by Feste's antics as Sir Topas, but begins to feel that the practical joke may get them into trouble. Feste talks with Malvolio again, this time as himself, and agrees to deliver a letter from Malvolio to Olivia. Malvolio is sure that this letter will prove that he is not mad.

2   *Sir Topas:* The topaz, a semiprecious stone, was believed to be a cure for lunacy. Shakespeare may have named Feste's priest for this reason. In Shakespeare's time, priests were often addressed as sir out of respect for their education; *curate:* assistant to a parish priest

3   *the whilst:* in the meantime

4   *dissemble:* disguise, conceal

5   *I would:* I wish; *dissembled:* concealed one's true self. Feste offers an offhand attack on the hypocrisy of the clergy.

6-7   *become the/function:* suit the role (of priest)

7   *lean:* thin. Students were notoriously poor – underfed and ragged

8   *said:* called

8-9   *good/housekeeper:* a hospitable person

9   *goes as fairly as to say:* is just as good as saying

10   *competitors:* associates, partners

12   *Bonos dies:* Good day (Latin). In the remainder of this speech, Feste is getting into his act by speaking like a scholar. The old hermit of Prague is Feste's own invention. Gorboduc was a legendary king of Britain. He may or may not have had a niece. The logic at the end is Feste's ironic comment on disguise and playing roles.

17   *To him:* Go to him.

18   *Peace in this prison:* This greeting, from the Elizabethan *Book of Common Prayer*, is required of any priest who enters a prison or hospital.

19   *knave:* lad (used as a term of affection for servants)

Stage direction – *Within:* Malvolio does not appear on stage, but speaks from the dark room in which he has been imprisoned. Directors often use a trapdoor in the stage floor to suggest that Malvolio has been locked in the cellars of Olivia's palace.

25   *Out, hyperbolical fiend:* Come out, boisterous devil. Feste addresses the devil who has supposedly possessed the body and soul of Malvolio.

Scene 2

A room in Olivia's house.

Enter Maria and Feste.

Going to see him in jail / Coherance

Maria: Nay, I prithee, put on this gown and this beard;
make him believe thou art Sir Topas the curate. Do it
quickly; I'll call Sir Toby the whilst.   [*Exit.*]

Dramatic Irony/Coherance Because Topas is a birth Stone.

Feste: Well, I'll put it on, and I will dissemble myself in't;
and I would I were the first that ever dissembled in
such a gown. I am not tall enough to become the
function well, nor lean enough to be thought a good
student; but to be said an honest man and a good
housekeeper goes as fairly as to say a careful man and
a great scholar. The competitors enter.   5

Topical Allusion To many priests are fake back then.

10

[*Enter Sir Toby and Maria.*]

Sir Toby: Jove bless thee, Master Parson.

Feste: Bonos dies, Sir Toby; for, as the old hermit of Prague,
that never saw pen and ink, very wittily said to a niece
of King Gorboduc, "That that is, is"; so I, being
Master Parson, am Master Parson; for, what is "that"
but "that", and "is" but "is"?   15

Legendary Allusion / not Science

Sir Toby: To him, Sir Topas.

Feste: What ho, I say! Peace in this prison!

Sir Toby: The knave counterfeits well; a good knave.

Malvolio: [*Within.*] Who calls there?   20

Feste: Sir Topas the curate, who comes to visit Malvolio
the lunatic.

Malvolio: Sir Topas, Sir Topas, good Sir Topas, go to my
lady.

Feste: Out, hyperbolical fiend! How vexest thou this man!   25
Talkest thou nothing but of ladies?

Sir Toby: Well said, Master Parson.

32   *modest:* moderate, mild

33   *use:* treat

34   *house:* room

36   *barricadoes:* barricades (which would prevent any light from entering the room)

37   *clearstories:* upper windows; *south north:* Feste continues to confuse Malvolio.

38   *lustrous:* shiny; *ebony:* a tropical tree with hard, black wood

39   *obstruction:* i.e., of the darkness

43   *puzzled:* lost

43-44   *the/Egyptians in their fog:* probably an allusion to the plague of darkness that Moses inflicted upon the Egyptians (Exodus 10: 21-23).

48   *Make the trial of it:* Test the truth of what I say; *constant question:* set problem

49   *Pythagoras:* a Greek philosopher who believed in reincarnation, a theory that, after death, a person's soul enters the body of another creature

51   *grandam:* grandmother; *haply:* perhaps

54   *I think nobly of the soul:* Malvolio is Christian, and rejects Pythagoras' philosophy.

57   *hold:* support, believe; *ere:* before

57-58   *allow/of thy wits:* certify your sanity

58   *woodcock:* a proverbially stupid bird

58-59   *dispossess:* dislodge

62   *for all waters:* ready for anything

65   *To him in thine own voice:* Go and speak to him in your own voice.

66-67   *I would . . . knavery:* I wish we could stop this joke.

67   *conveniently delivered:* released without fuss

Malvolio: Sir Topas, never was man thus wronged. Good
Sir Topas, do not think I am mad; they have laid me
here in hideous darkness.

Feste: Fie, thou dishonest Satan! I call thee by the most
modest terms; for I am one of those gentle ones that
will use the devil himself with courtesy. Sayest thou that
house is dark?

Malvolio: As hell, Sir Topas.

Feste: Why, it hath bay windows transparent as barricadoes,
and the clearstories towards the south north are as
lustrous as ebony; and yet complainest thou of
obstruction?

Malvolio: I am not mad, Sir Topas; I say to you, this house   40
is dark.

Feste: Madman, thou errest. I say, there is no darkness but
ignorance, in which thou art more puzzled than the
Egyptians in their fog.

Malvolio: I say, this house is as dark as ignorance, though   45
ignorance were as dark as hell; and I say, there was
never man thus abused. I am no more mad than you
are. Make the trial of it in any constant question.

Feste: What is the opinion of Pythagoras concerning wild
fowl?   50

Malvolio: That the soul of our grandam might haply inhabit
a bird.

Feste: What thinkest thou of his opinion?

Malvolio: I think nobly of the soul, and no way approve
his opinion.   55

Feste: Fare thee well. Remain thou still in darkness. Thou
shalt hold the opinion of Pythagoras ere I will allow
of thy wits; and fear to kill a woodcock, lest thou dispossess the soul of thy grandam. Fare thee well.

Malvolio: Sir Topas, Sir Topas!

Sir Toby: My most exquisite Sir Topas!

Feste: Nay, I am for all waters.

Maria: Thou mightst have done this without thy beard and
gown: he sees thee not.

Sir Toby: To him in thine own voice, and bring me word   65
how thou findest him. I would we were well rid of
this knavery. If he may be conveniently delivered,

68   *offence:* trouble

70   *upshot:* conclusion, end; *by and by:* soon

72-79   *Hey, Robin . . . She loves another:* These are lines from a song
that was very popular in Shakespeare's day.

75   *perdy:* by God (French *par Dieu*)

80-81   *as ever thou . . . hand:* if you want to do me a favour that I will
reward you for

81   *help me to:* fetch me

86   *how fell . . . wits?:* How did you happen to lose your five wits?
In Elizabethan times, the five wits were considered to be
common sense, imagination, fantasy, judgement, and
memory.

87   *notoriously abused:* shamefully ill-treated

89   *But as well?:* only as well (i.e., you have no more wit than a
fool)

91   *propertied me:* treated me as though I were an object or
property rather than a person

93   *face:* boldly insists that I have lost my wits

94   *Advise you:* be careful, watch out

96   *Endeavour thyself:* try

96-97   *vain bibble/babble:* useless nonsense

99   *words:* conversation

100   *God be wi' you:* God be with you.

103   *shent:* scolded, rebuked

I would he were, for I am now so far in offence
with my niece that I cannot pursue with any safety
this sport to the upshot. Come by and by to my   70
chamber.   [*Exeunt Sir Toby and Maria.*]
Feste: Hey, Robin, jolly Robin,
   Tell me how thy lady does.
Malvolio: Fool!
Feste: My lady is unkind, perdy.   75
Malvolio: Fool!
Feste: Alas, why is she so?
Malvolio: Fool, I say!
Feste: She loves another—Who calls, ha?
Malvolio: Good fool, as ever thou wilt deserve well at my   80
   hand, help me to a candle, and pen, ink, and paper. As
   I am a gentleman, I will live to be thankful to thee
   for't.
Feste: Master Malvolio?
Malvolio: Ay, good fool.   85
Feste: Alas, sir, how fell you besides your five wits?
Malvolio: Fool, there was never man so notoriously abused.
   I am as well in my wits, fool, as thou art.
Feste: But as well? Then you are mad indeed, if you be no
   better in your wits than a fool.   90
Malvolio: They have here propertied me; keep me in dark-
   ness, send ministers to me, asses, and do all they can
   to face me out of my wits.
Feste: Advise you what you say; the minister is here.
   Malvolio, Malvolio, thy wits the heavens restore!   95
   Endeavour thyself to sleep, and leave thy vain bibble
   babble.
Malvolio: Sir Topas!
Feste: Maintain no words with him, good fellow. Who, I,
   sir? Not I, sir. God be wi' you, good Sir Topas. Marry,   100
   amen. I will, sir, I will.
Malvolio: Fool, fool, fool, I say!
Feste: Alas, sir, be patient. What say you, sir? I am shent
   for speaking to you.
Malvolio: Good fool, help me to some light and some paper. 105
   I tell thee, I am as well in my wits as any man in
   Illyria.

108   *Well-a-day that you were:* Alas! If only you were

110   *convey:* deliver; *set down:* write

111   *advantage:* reward

114   *counterfeit:* pretend

118   *requite:* repay

120-131   *I am . . . devil:* Feste's song is like those found in morality plays of the 15th and 16th centuries. The *vice*, a character who carried a wooden sword (*dagger of lath*), would cut the devil's nails and drive him from the stage. Shakespeare's audience would have been quite familiar with the topic of the song.

121   *anon:* immediately

123   *In a trice:* in a flash

124   *old:* familiar

130   *Pare:* cut

131   *goodman:* good master, equivalent to the modern *mister*

Feste: Well-a-day that you were, sir!

Malvolio: By this hand, I am. Good fool, some ink, paper, and light; and convey what I will set down to my lady. It shall advantage thee more than ever the bearing of letter did.

Feste: I will help you to't. But tell me true, are you not mad indeed? Or do you but counterfeit?

Malvolio: Believe me, I am not; I tell thee true. 115

Feste: Nay, I'll ne'er believe a madman till I see his brains. I will fetch you light and paper and ink.

Malvolio: Fool, I'll requite it in the highest degree. I prithee, be gone.

Feste: I am gone, sir, 120
　　　And anon, sir,
　　I'll be with you again,
　　　In a trice,
　　　Like to the old Vice,
　　Your need to sustain; 125
　　Who, with dagger of lath,
　　In his rage and his wrath,
　　　Cries, aha! to the devil:
　　Like a mad lad,
　　Pare thy nails, dad; 130
　　　Adieu, goodman devil. [*Exit.*]

Handwritten annotations:

It will be more to your advantage that any other letter that he has carried. (He will get lots of money)

I will reward you with lots of money

rhyming couplet

rhyming couplet.

Bye Bye Mr. Devil!

201

Act 4, Scene 2: Activities

1. As Malvolio, write a letter to Olivia in which you complain about your unfair treatment at the hands of Toby and the others. Remember that Malvolio still believes that he has been following the instructions of Olivia's love letter.

2. Write a scene in which Maria and Toby discuss and decide that the joke on Malvolio has been carried far enough. If you wish, you could write the scene in the language of today, but remain true to the character and personalities that Shakespeare has developed.

3. In a small group, brainstorm a list of some television shows or movies you have seen in which a character uses a disguise. Was the disguise used for a serious or comic purpose? Why do you think Shakespeare disguised Feste in this scene? Use your answers to these questions to reach some conclusions about the purposes of disguise in drama.

4. Feste's portrayal of a clergyman pokes fun at the assumed solemnity and pomposity of some churchmen. What other figures of authority or persons of importance in our society are the frequent targets of satire? Consider some specific examples, drawing upon books, films, television shows, music videos, radio, and other plays. With a partner, discuss why you think people enjoy a good comic "put-down".

For the next scene . . .

How might you react to a proposal of marriage from a wealthy stranger? What are some of the thoughts you might have? How would you respond?

Act 4, Scene 3

In this scene . . .

Sebastian is waiting in Olivia's garden for her and is confused. He doesn't know where Antonio has gone, and he can't figure out why Olivia admires him so much. Olivia finds him and insists that she and Sebastian go with her priest to make a formal engagement until preparations for their marriage can be arranged. Sebastian thinks that either he himself or Olivia must be mad, but he agrees to Olivia's proposal.

6   *there he was:* he had been there; *credit:* report

7   *range:* wander about

9   *my soul . . . sense:* My reason agrees with the evidence of my senses.

12   *instance:* precedent; *discourse:* explanation

14   *wrangle:* argue

15   *trust:* belief

17   *sway her house:* manage her household: *followers:* servants

18   *Take and . . . dispatch:* manage her affairs

19   *With such . . . bearing:* in such a calm, careful, and thorough way

21   *deceivable:* deceptive

24   *chantry by:* nearby chapel

26   *Plight me . . . faith:* Give me total assurance of your commitment.

27   *jealous:* possessive, anxious; *doubtful:* insecure

29   *Whiles:* until; *come to note:* become public knowledge

Scene 3

Olivia's garden.

Enter Sebastian~ (*handwritten: ring,*)

(handwritten annotation: This is really happening. She did give him the pearl / ring.)

Sebastian: This is the air; that is the glorious sun;
This pearl she gave me, I do feel't and see't;
And though 'tis wonder that enwraps me thus,
Yet 'tis not madness. Where's Antonio, then?
I could not find him at the Elephant; *(handwritten: coherance)*   5
Yet there he was; and there I found this credit,
That he did range the town to seek me out.
His counsel now might do me golden service; *(handwritten: metaphor personification. He wants advice.)*
For though my soul disputes well with my sense; *(handwritten: personlfication)*
That this may be some error, but no madness. *(handwritten: metaphoric)*
Yet doth this accident and flood of fortune *(handwritten: Everything good coming like a flood. She Keeps)*
So far exceed all instance, all discourse,
That I am ready to distrust mine eyes,
And wrangle with my reason, that persuades me *(handwritten: Either I'm mad or she is but she cant be mad because she rules the house)*
To any other trust but that I am mad,   15
Or else the lady's mad; yet, if 'twere so,
She could not sway her house, command her followers,
Take and give back affairs and their dispatch
With such a smooth, discreet, and stable bearing
As I perceive she does. There's something in't   20
That is deceivable. But here the lady comes.
[*Enter Olivia and Priest.*]
Olivia: Blame not this haste of mine. If you mean well,
Now go with me and with this holy man
Into the chantry by. There, before him, *(handwritten: chantry = that sacred roof.)*
And underneath that consecrated roof,   25
Plight me the full assurance of your faith,
That my most jealous and too doubtful soul
May live at peace. He shall conceal it
Whiles you are willing it shall come to note,

(handwritten left margin: soliloquy)

205

30   *What time:* at which time; *our celebration keep:* celebrate our marriage

31   *According to my birth:* in the style that someone of my social rank and position is due

35   *fairly note:* look favourably on

What time we will our celebration keep   30
According to my birth. What do you say?
Sebastian: I'll follow this good man, and go with you;
  And, having sworn truth, ever will be true.
Olivia: Then lead the way, good father; and heavens so
    shine,
That they may fairly note this act of mine!   [*Exeunt.*]   35

Act 4, Scene 3: Activities

1. At the end of this scene, Sebastian agrees to Olivia's proposal of marriage even though he reveals his uncertainty in his soliloquy at the beginning of the scene.

   Suppose that Shakespeare had written a speech at the end of the scene in which Sebastian decides to accept the proposal. It could be either a soliloquy or a direct comment to Olivia preceding line 31. Compose either of these speeches in prose or verse according to your understanding of Sebastian's character.

2. Debate in parliamentary style:

   Resolved that Sebastian is too spontaneous and impetuous for his own good.

Act 4: Consider the Whole Act

1. Create a television news feature based on the accounts and rumours of "strange events" at Olivia's house. You might include interviews with characters who are involved in the events or with others who might have witnessed them. You can assume that the average Illyrian is hungry for gossip about the lives of rich and famous citizens.

2. Compile a list of words and phrases to describe the character of Sebastian as he appears in Scenes 1 and 3 of this act.

   Consider how Viola might have reacted under circumstances similar to the ones in which Sebastian found himself. In what ways is Sebastian unlike his sister? How is he similar? Which of the two characters do you admire more? Compare the reasons for your preference with those of other students in the class, particularly with classmates of the opposite sex.

3. At this stage of the play, what are the chances for a happy ending? In a small group, discuss your responses to the following questions:
   - How might Sebastian's presence in Illyria contribute to a happy ending?
   - How does Sebastian's character suggest he will aid in the resolution of the conflicts?
   - How does Toby offer hope for reconciliation within Olivia's household?
   - What problems remain to be solved before *everyone* can live "happily ever after"?
   - Which of these problems poses the greatest threat to a happy ending?

4. Select a character from one of the scenes in this act, design a full-colour costume for him or her that would satisfy the dramatic requirements of the scene, and draw a sketch of your costume. Be sure to consider not only the personality and mood of the character, but also the physical demands placed upon the actor playing the role.

   To your colour sketch, attach small samples of the fabrics that you recommend. Be prepared to explain to your classmates your choices of colour, style, and detail. Remember that a professional designer is expected to estimate the cost of a costume.

5. As Olivia, write a diary entry in which you reflect upon the "madness" of the past few days and express your feelings about your recent engagement.

For the next scene . . .

Recall a situation in which you felt yourself betrayed by someone whom you loved or trusted. Did you satisfy your sense of justice through revenge? through compromise? What determined the course of action you took?

Act 5, Scene 1

In this scene . . .

When Viola and Sebastian finally meet, the many cases of mistaken identity are resolved at last. Malvolio is released and is given an opportunity to speak. The play ends with a promise of marriage and a song from Feste.

1   *his letter:* i.e., Malvolio's letter to Olivia

5-6   *This is . . . again:* Fabian alludes here to the story of Queen
          Elizabeth I and Dr. Bulleyn, who was very fond of his dog.
          The queen asked Dr. Bulleyn to grant her one request and she
          promised, in return, to grant a request of him. The queen
          asked for the dog. The doctor gave it to her and then asked
          her to give it back.

7   *Belong you . . . Olivia:* Are you members of Olivia's household?

8   *trappings:* decorations, ornaments

10   *for:* because of

15   *make an ass of me:* i.e., they make a fool of me with their lies

18   *abused:* deceived with flattery

18-19   *conclusions to/be as kisses:* if conclusions may be compared
          to kisses. Perhaps Feste is thinking of the lover who says
          "No, no" when asked for a kiss. The two negatives cancel,
          and the other lover hears "Yes." Or Feste could be playing
          with the idea that four lips make up two mouths that join in a
          single kiss.

24   *friends:* i.e., one of those who flatter me

26   *But that:* except for the fact that; *double-dealing:* both "giving
          twice" and "duplicity" or "deceit"; *I would:* I wish

Act 5, Scene 1

The street before Olivia's house.

Enter Feste and Fabian.

Fabian: Now, as thou lovest me, let me see his letter. Coherence

Feste: Good Master Fabian, grant me another request.

Fabian: Anything.

Feste: Do not desire to see this letter.

Fabian: This is, to give a dog, and in recompense desire   5
    my dog again. Topical Allusion

[*Enter Duke Orsino, Viola, Curio, and Lords.*]

Duke: Belong you to the Lady Olivia, friends?

Feste: Ay, sir, we are some of her trappings.

Duke: I know thee well. How dost thou, my good fellow?

Feste: Truly, sir, the better for my foes and the worse for my   10
    friends. Friends: Aren't truthful / Enemies: Are honest

Duke: Just the contrary, the better for thy friends.

Feste: No, sir, the worse.

Duke: How can that be?

Feste: Marry, sir, they praise me and make an ass of me;   15
    now my foes tell me plainly I am an ass: so that by my
    foes, sir, I profit in the knowledge of myself, and
    by my friends I am abused: so that, conclusions to
    be as kisses, if your four negatives make your two
    affirmatives, why then, the worse for my friends and   20
    the better for my foes.

Duke: Why, this is excellent.

Feste: By my troth, sir, no, though it please you to be one
    of my friends. Wants money

Duke: Thou shalt not be the worse for me. There's gold. ·   25

Feste: But that it would be double-dealing, sir, I would you
    could make it another.

28   *ill counsel:* bad advice

29-30 *Put your . . . it:* To put something in your pocket meant to forget something. Feste asks Orsino to forget his dignity and social breeding (*grace*). At the same time, Feste puns on *grace* as generosity: show your usual generosity by reaching into your pocket and finding me a coin.

33   *Primo, secundo, tertio:* first, second, third (Latin); *play:* game

34   *triplex:* triple time in music

35   *tripping measure:* skipping rhythm; *Saint Bennet:* the church of St. Benedict, very near Shakespeare's Globe Theatre

37   *fool:* trick; *throw:* throw of the dice

40   *bounty:* generosity

45   *anon:* soon

49   *Vulcan:* the Roman god of fire and blacksmiths

50   *bawbling:* insignificant

51   *shallow draught:* very light in tonnage or mass. *Draught* refers to the depth of water needed to keep a particular ship afloat; *bulk unprizable:* of no value, not worth capturing as a prize

52   *scathful:* destructive; *grapple:* close encounter

53   *bottom:* vessel

54   *very envy . . . loss:* everyone who had reason to envy him (i.e., his enemies) and the voices of those who lost the battle

55   *Cried fame and honour on him:* praised and honoured him

57   *took:* captured in battle; *fraught:* freight, cargo; *Candy:* Candia (now called Crete)

60   *desperate of shame and state:* recklessly disregarding his previous shameful behaviour and the danger of being a wanted man

61   *brabble:* brawl; *apprehend:* arrest

62   *drew on my side:* drew his sword to protect me

63   *in conclusion:* later on; *put strange speech upon me:* spoke to me very strangely

64   *distraction:* madness

66   *to their mercies:* into the hands of those

Duke: Oh, you give me ill counsel.
Feste: Put your grace in your pocket, sir, for this once, and
    let your flesh and blood obey it. 30
Duke: Well, I will be so much a sinner, to be a double-
    dealer; there's another.
Feste: Primo, secundo, tertio, is a good play; and the old
    saying is, the third pays for all. The triplex, sir, is a
    good tripping measure; or the bells of Saint Bennet, 35
    sir, may put you in mind; one, two, three.
Duke: You can fool no more money out of me at this throw.
    If you will let your lady know I am here to speak
    with her, and bring her along with you, it may awake
    my bounty further. 40
Feste: Marry, sir, lullaby to your bounty till I come again.
    I go, sir, but I would not have you to think that my
    desire of having is the sin of covetousness; but, as you
    say, sir, let your bounty take a nap, I will awake it
    anon. [*Exit.*] 45
Viola: Here comes the man, sir, that did rescue me.
    [*Enter Antonio and Officers.*]
Duke: That face of his I do remember well;
    Yet, when I saw it last it was besmear'd
    As black as Vulcan in the smoke of war.
    A bawbling vessel was he captain of, 50
    For shallow draught and bulk unprizable,
    With which such scathful grapple did he make
    With the most noble bottom of our fleet,
    That very envy and the tongue of loss
    Cried fame and honour on him. What's the matter? 55
First Officer: Orsino, this is that Antonio
    That took the Phœnix and her fraught from Candy;
    And this is he that did the Tiger board,
    When your young nephew Titus lost his leg.
    Here in the streets, desperate of shame and state, 60
    In private brabble did we apprehend him.
Viola: He did me kindness, sir, drew on my side;
    But in conclusion put strange speech upon me
    I know not what 'twas but distraction.
Duke: Notable pirate! Thou salt-water thief! 65
    What foolish boldness brought thee to their mercies,

67	*in terms . . . dear:* in such bloody and grievous circumstances
69	*Be pleased that I:* please, let me; *shake off:* reject
71	*on base and ground enough:* with very good reason
72	*A witchcraft drew me hither:* I came here because I was bewitched.
73	*ingrateful:* ungrateful
74	*rude:* rough
75	*redeem:* save, rescue; *a wreck past hope:* a hopeless wreck
77	*retention:* reservation (i.e., I held nothing back)
78	*All his in dedication:* I devoted myself to him completely.
79	*pure for his love:* entirely for my love of him
80	*adverse:* hostile
81	*beset:* attacked
82	*Where being apprehended:* when I was arrested
83	*partake with me in danger:* share the danger with me
84	*face me out of his acquaintance:* brazenly deny that he knew me
85	*grew . . . removèd thing:* acted as though he had not seen me for twenty years
86	*While one could wink:* in the wink of an eye; *denied me:* refused to give me
87	*recommended to his use:* persuaded him to take for his own use
91	*No interim:* without interim or break; *vacancy:* space
92	*keep company:* stay together
95	*tended upon:* attended on, served
96	*anon:* soon
97	*What would my lord:* what would you like; *but that he may not have:* with the exception of that which I will not give him (i.e., my love)
98	*seem serviceable:* be of some use or assistance

Whom thou, in terms so bloody and so dear,
Hast made thine enemies?
Antonio: Orsino, noble sir,
Be pleased that I shake off these names you give me.
Antonio never yet was thief or pirate,   70
Though I confess, on base and ground enough,
Orsino's enemy. A witchcraft drew me hither.
That most ingrateful boy there by your side,
From the rude sea's enraged and foamy mouth
Did I redeem; a wreck past hope he was.   75
His life I gave him and did thereto add
My love, without retention or restraint,
All his in dedication; for his sake
Did I expose myself, pure for his love,
Into the danger of this adverse town;   80
Drew to defend him when he was beset:
Where being apprehended, his false cunning,
Not meaning to partake with me in danger,
Taught him to face me out of his acquaintance,
And grew a twenty years removed thing   85
While one could wink; denied me mine own purse,
Which I had recommended to his use
Not half an hour before.
Viola: How can this be?
Duke: When came he to this town?
Antonio: To-day, my lord; and for three months before, 90
No interim, not a minute's vacancy,
Both day and night did we keep company.
[*Enter Olivia and Attendants.*]
Duke: Here comes the countess; now heaven walks on earth.
But for thee, fellow,—fellow, thy words are madness.
Three months this youth hath tended upon me;   95
But more of that anon. Take him aside.
Olivia: What would my lord, but that he may not have,
Wherein Olivia may seem serviceable?
Cesario, you do not keep promise with me.
Viola: Madam!   100
Duke: Gracious Olivia,—
Olivia: What do you say, Cesario? Good my lord,—
Viola: My lord would speak; my duty hushes me.

104   *aught to the old tune:* like the same old romantic stuff (which I've heard constantly from you)

105   *fat and fulsome:* gross and offensive

106   *howling:* i.e., of dogs

109   *ingrate:* ungrateful; *unauspicious:* unfavourable

111   *That e'er devotion tender'd:* that were ever offered in devotion

112   *Even what:* whatever; *become him:* suit him, make him attractive

114-115 *Like to . . . love?:* Orsino alludes here to the story of Thyamis and Chariclea. Thyamis, a robber chief, kidnapped the princess Chariclea and retreated to a cave, where he was attacked by other robbers. He tried to kill Chariclea so that his attackers couldn't have her; however, in the darkness of the cave, he killed another woman instead.

116   *savours nobly:* is not without nobility; *hear me this:* Listen to what I have to say.

117   *non-regardance:* neglect; *that:* since

119   *screws:* forces, pries; *true:* rightful

120   *marble-breasted:* hard-hearted (like a marble statue)

121   *minion:* darling

122   *tender dearly:* hold in affection

124   *in his master's spite:* in defiance of his master. Orsino seems as angry with Viola/Cesario as with Olivia.

125   *ripe in mischief:* ready to inflict injury

127   *a raven's heart within a dove:* a cruel heart within a beautiful body

128   *jocund:* happy, cheerful; *apt;* ready

129   *To do you rest:* to bring you satisfaction and peace of mind

132   *by all mores:* by all such comparisons

133-134 *If I do . . . love:* If I am dishonest (*If I do feign*), I call on the gods (*you witnesses above*) to punish me with death for being disloyal to the one I love (*for tainting of my love*).

135   *Ay me, detested:* Oh, I am cursed; *beguiled:* tricked, deceived

Olivia: If it be aught to the old tune, my lord,
   It is as fat and fulsome to mine ear   105
   As howling after music.
Duke: Still so cruel?
Olivia: Still so constant, lord.
Duke: What, to perverseness? You uncivil lady,
   To whose ingrate and unauspicious altars
   My soul the faithfull'st offerings hath breathed out   110
   That e'er devotion tender'd! What shall I do?
Olivia: Even what it please my lord, that shall become him.
Duke: Why should I not, had I the heart to do it,
   Like to the Egyptian thief at point of death,
   Kill what I love?—a savage jealousy   115
   That sometime savours nobly. But hear me this:
   Since you to non-regardance cast my faith,
   And that I partly know the instrument
   That screws me from my true place in your favour,
   Live you the marble-breasted tyrant still;   120
   But this your minion, whom I know you love,
   And whom, by heaven I swear, I tender dearly,
   Him will I tear out of that cruel eye,
   Where he sits crowned in his master's spite.
   Come, boy, with me; my thoughts are ripe in mischief. 125
   I'll sacrifice the lamb that I do love,
   To spite a raven's heart within a dove.
Viola: And I, most jocund, apt, and willingly,
   To do you rest, a thousand deaths would die.
Olivia: Where goes Cesario?
Viola: After him I love
   More than I love these eyes, more than my life,
   More, by all mores, than e'er I shall love wife.
   If I do feign, you witnesses above
   Punish my life for tainting of my love!
Olivia: Ay me, detested! How am I beguiled!
Viola: Who does beguile you? Who does do you wrong?
Olivia: Hast thou forgot thyself? Is it so long?
   Call forth the holy father.
Duke: Come, away!
Olivia: Whither, my lord? Cesario, husband, stay.
Duke: Husband!

141 *sirrah:* customary form of address to a menial servant

142 *the baseness of thy fear:* your despicable cowardice

143 *strangle thy propriety:* deny your true identity

144 *take thy fortunes up:* accept the position that your good luck has provided

145 *that:* what

146 *as that thou fear'st:* as the man you are afraid of (i.e., Orsino)

147 *charge:* order

148 *unfold:* reveal, disclose

149 *in darkness:* hidden; *occasion:* circumstance

151 *newly pass'd:* recently taken place

153 *joinder:* joining

154 *Attested:* validated; *close of lips:* kiss (the closing together of lips)

155 *interchangement:* exchange

157 *Seal'd in my function:* made official by my position as priest

160 *dissembling:* deceitful; *cub:* young fox. (*Cub* may refer to the young of many animals, but the fox is proverbially cunning and sly.)

161 *sow'd:* planted; *a grizzle on thy case?:* gray hairs on your skin

162 *craft:* cunning, duplicity

163 *trip:* a leg movement in wrestling. (Orsino suggests that Cesario might become too clever and trip himself up in his own deceit.)

167 *Hold little faith:* keep at least a little faith

169 *presently:* immediately

172 *coxcomb:* head. A *coxcomb* is actually a fool's cap, resembling the crest of a rooster. The word is most often a synonym for fool, but can mean simply head.

Olivia:　　　　　Ay, husband: can he that deny?　　　140
Duke: Her husband, sirrah! *insulting name/ Lower Class*
Viola:　　　　　　No, my lord, not I.
Olivia: Alas, it is the baseness of thy fear
　That makes thee strangle thy propriety.
　Fear not, Cesario; take thy fortunes up;
　Be that thou know'st thou art, and then thou art 　145
　As great as that thou fear'st.

If you marry me you will be at the enemies rank: count/countess

　[*Enter Priest.*]　　　Oh, welcome, father!
　Father, I charge thee, by thy reverence,
　Here to unfold, though lately we intended
　To keep in darkness what occasion now *you Olivia what you promised to keep secret.*
　Reveals before 'tis ripe, what thou dost know　150
　Hath newly pass'd between this youth and me.
Priest: A contract of eternal bond of love,
　Confirm'd by mutual joinder of your hands, *Tells them what*
　Attested by the holy close of lips, *happened 2 hours*
　Strengthen'd by interchangement of your rings; *ago.*　155
　And all the ceremony of this compact
　Seal'd in my function, by my testimony:
　Since when, my watch hath told me, toward my grave
　I have travell'd but two hours.
Duke: O thou dissembling cub! What wilt thou be　*Time Sews grey*　160
　When time hath sow'd a grizzle on thy case? *hair on your face.*
　Or will not else thy craft so quickly grow,
　That thine own trip shall be thine overthrow? *+ take Olivia with*
　Farewell, and take her; but direct thy feet *Go you tramp* *Go*
　Where thou and I henceforth may never meet *I will never see*　165
Viola: My lord, I do protest— *you again*
Olivia:　　　　　Oh, do not swear!
　Hold little faith, though thou hast too much fear. *you*
　[*Enter Sir Andrew.*] *Beleive I will protect you*
Sir Andrew: For the love of God, a surgeon! Send one *Sir toby has*
　presently to Sir Toby. *a bloody head.*
Olivia: What's the matter? 　170
Sir Andrew: He has broke my head across and has given *Sir Andrew has*
　Sir Toby a bloody coxcomb too. For the love of God, *one two. but*
　your help! I had rather than forty pound I were at *he is thinking about Sir Toby. (That's a*
　home. *I'd rather go home than get 40 dollars. hands.*
Olivia: Who has done this, Sir Andrew?　　175 *change).*

177   *incardinate:* Sir Andrew means incarnate, in the flesh.

179   *'Od's lifelings:* By God's little lives

180   *that that I did:* what I did; *set on to do't:* persuaded to do it

184   *bespake you fair:* answered you courteously

186   *set nothing by:* think nothing of

187   *halting:* limping

189   *tickled:* treated; *othergates:* otherwise, in a different way

192   *That's all one:* that doesn't matter; *has:* he has

192-193 *there's the end/on't:* That's all there is to it.

193   *Sot:* fool and drunkard

194   *an hour agone:* for the past hour

195   *set:* closed

196   *passy measures pavin: passamezzo pavan,* a slow and stately dance of eight bars. Toby's meaning is unclear, but the reference was certainly suggested by the surgeon's drunkenness at eight in the morning.

200   *we'll be dressed:* We'll have our wounds dressed.

203   *gull:* dupe, idiot

204   *hurt:* wound; *looked to:* looked after

206   *the brother of my blood:* my own relative

207   *with wit and safety:* with intelligent concern for my own safety

208   *You throw . . . me:* You are staring at me very oddly.

210   *even for:* especially because of

211   *but so late ago:* so very recently

212   *habit:* way of dressing

213   *perspective:* optical illusion (like that produced by a stereoscope, which brings together two flat images into a single three-dimensional one)

Sir Andrew: The count's gentleman, one Cesario. We took
him for a coward, but he's the very devil incardinate.

[handwritten: Cesario is a living devil.]

Duke: My gentleman, Cesario?
Sir Andrew: 'Od's lifelings! Here he is! You broke my head
for nothing; and that that I did, I was set on to do't   180
by Sir Toby.

[handwritten: what I did was because Sir Toby told me]

Viola: Why do you speak to me? I never hurt you:
You drew your sword upon me without cause;
But I bespake you fair, and hurt you not.

[handwritten: I didn't hurt you. I spoke nicely to you.]

Sir Andrew: If a bloody coxcomb be a hurt, you have hurt   185
me: I think you set nothing by a bloody coxcomb.
[*Enter Sir Toby and Feste.*] Here comes Sir Toby halting; you shall hear more: but if he had not been in
drink, he would have tickled you othergates than he
did.   190
Duke: How now, gentleman! How is't with you?
Sir Toby: That's all one; has hurt me, and there's the end
on't. Sot, didst see Dick surgeon, sot?

[handwritten: Where is the surgeon.]

Feste: Oh, he's drunk, Sir Toby, an hour agone; his eyes
were set at eight i' the morning.   195

[handwritten: DRUNK?]

Sir Toby: Then he's a rogue, and a passy measures pavin.
I hate a drunken rogue.
Olivia: Away with him! Who hath made this havoc with
them?
Sir Andrew: I'll help you, Sir Toby, because we'll be dressed   200
together.

[handwritten: Dressing the wound.]

Sir Toby: Will you help? an ass-head and a coxcomb and a
knave, a thin-faced knave, a gull!

[handwritten: Swearing at Sir Andrew in every possible way.]

Olivia: Get him to bed, and let his hurt be looked to.
[*Exeunt Feste, Fabian, Sir Toby, and Sir Andrew.*]
[*Enter Sebastian.*]
Sebastian: I am sorry, madam, I have hurt your kinsman;   205
But, had it been the brother of my blood,
I must have done no less with wit and safety.

[handwritten: I would have done this because of my brother he did.]

You throw a strange regard upon me, and by that
I do perceive it hath offended you.
Pardon me, sweet one, even for the vows   210
We made each other but so late ago.
Duke: One face, one voice, one habit, and two persons,
A natural perspective, that is, and is not!

[handwritten: Illusion]

223

215   *rack'd:* kept me on the rack. The rack was a wooden wheel on which a person was tied and stretched in order to force a confession.

217   *Fear'st thou that:* Do you doubt it?

218   *made division of yourself?:* divided yourself

219   *cleft:* cut, split

221   *wonderful:* amazing

222   *Do I stand there?:* Is that me standing over there? (Sebastian has just caught sight of Cesario at the other end of the stage.)

223-224 *Nor can . . . everywhere:* and I am not like a god who can be everywhere at the same time

225   *blind:* merciless, indiscriminate

226   *Of charity:* for charity's sake, out of simple kindness; *kin:* relation

227   *What countryman?:* What is your nationality?

230   *So went he suited:* He was clothed like this when he went.

231   *If spirits . . . suit:* if devils have the power to assume the shape and clothing of human beings

231   *fright:* frighten, terrify; *spirit:* human soul. (Sebastian puns on Viola's use of *spirits* in line 231.)

233-234 *am in that . . . participate:* clothed in the body that I, like other human beings, acquired at birth

235   *Were you:* if you were; *as the rest goes even:* as everything (other than your clothing) seems to suggest

242   *record:* memory; *lively:* vivid

243   *mortal act:* life

245   *lets:* interferes

246   *But:* except; *usurp'd:* used without authority; here, simply inappropriate

248   *cohere and jump:* fall together and fit exactly

251   *Where:* in whose possession; *maiden weeds:* female clothing

Sebastian: Antonio, O my dear Antonio!
  How have the hours rack'd and tortured me   215
  Since I have lost thee!
Antonio: Sebastian are you?
Sebastian: Fear'st thou that, Antonio?
Antonio: How have you made division of yourself?
  An apple, cleft in two, is not more twin
  Than these two creatures. Which is Sebastian?   220
Olivia: Most wonderful!
Sebastian: Do I stand there? I never had a brother;
  Nor can there be that deity in my nature,
  Of here and everywhere. I had a sister,
  Whom the blind waves and surges have devour'd.   225
  Of charity, what kin are you to me?
  What countryman? What name? What parentage?
Viola: Of Messaline. Sebastian was my father;
  Such a Sebastian was my brother too,
  So went he suited to his watery tomb.   230
  If spirits can assume both form and suit,
  You come to fright us.
Sebastian: A spirit I am indeed;
  But am in that dimension grossly clad
  Which from the womb I did participate.
  Were you a woman, as the rest goes even,   235
  I should my tears let fall upon your cheek,
  And say, "Thrice-welcome, drowned Viola!"
Viola: My father had a mole upon his brow.
Sebastian: And so had mine.
Viola: And died that day when Viola from her birth   240
  Had number'd thirteen years.
Sebastian: Oh, that record is lively in my soul!
  He finished indeed his mortal act
  That day that made my sister thirteen years.
Viola: If nothing lets to make us happy both   245
  But this my masculine usurp'd attire,
  Do not embrace me till each circumstance
  Of place, time, fortune, do cohere and jump
  That I am Viola: which to confirm,
  I'll bring you to a captain in this town,   250
  Where lie my maiden weeds; by whose gentle help

253	*All the . . . since:* everything that has happened to me since that time
254	*been between:* has to do with
255	*been mistook:* made a mistake
256	*nature to . . . that:* Nature followed her usual pattern.
257	*contracted:* married
258	*therein, by my life, deceived:* cheated in that respect
259	*maid:* virgin male
260	*amazed:* worried; *right noble is his blood:* He is of true and noble birth.
261	*glass:* the *natural perspective* of line 213
262	*happy wreck:* lucky shipwreck
264	*like to me:* as much as me
265	*over-swear:* swear again and again
267	*As doth . . . fire:* as the sun (*that orbed continent*) keeps its fire
269	*weeds:* clothing
271	*action:* legal charge
272	*in durance:* under arrest; *at Malvolio's suit:* at the request of Malvolio
274	*enlarge:* release
276	*much distract:* very disturbed (in his mind)
277-278	*A most . . . his:* My own madness, which has drawn (*extracted*) all other concerns from my mind, has obviously removed (*banished*) his madness from my memory.
280	*he holds . . . end:* He keeps the devil at a safe distance.
281	*case:* condition
283-284	*as a madman's epistles . . . delivered:* Since there is no truth (*gospel*) in a madman's letters, it doesn't really matter (*it skills not*) when they are read aloud (*delivered*).
286	*Look:* prepare; *edified:* informed
286-287	*delivers/the madman:* reads the words of a madman

I was preserved to serve this noble count.
All the occurrence of my fortune since
Hath been between this lady and this lord.
Sebastian: [*To Olivia.*] So comes it, lady, you have been
  mistook;   255
But nature to her bias drew in that.
You would have been contracted to a maid;
Nor are you therein, by my life, deceived;
You are betroth'd both to a maid and man.
Duke: Be not amazed; right noble is his blood.   260
If this be so, as yet the glass seems true,
I shall have share in this most happy wreck.
[*To Viola.*] Boy, thou hast said to me a thousand times
Thou never shouldst love woman like to me.
Viola: And all those sayings will I over-swear;   265
And all those swearings keep as true in soul
As doth that orbed continent the fire
That severs day from night.
Duke: Give me thy hand;
And let me see thee in thy woman's weeds.
Viola: The captain that did bring me first on shore   270
Hath my maid's garments. He upon some action
Is now in durance, at Malvolio's suit,
A gentleman, and follower of my lady's.
Olivia: He shall enlarge him. Fetch Malvolio hither;
And yet, alas, now I remember me,   275
They say, poor gentleman, he's much distract.
[*Re-enter Feste with a letter, and Fabian.*]
A most extracting frenzy of mine own
From my remembrance clearly banish'd his.
How does he, sirrah?
Feste: Truly, madam, he holds Beelzebub at the stave's end   280
  as well as a man in his case may do: has here writ a
  letter to you; I should have given't to you to-day
  morning, but as a madman's epistles are no gospels,
  so it skills not much when they are delivered.
Olivia: Open't, and read it.   285
Feste: Look then to be well edified when the fool delivers
  the madman. [*Reads.*] *By the Lord, madam,*—

289   *an:* if

290   *allow Vox:* let me use the proper voice

291   *i' thy right wits:* in a proper state of mind

292   *madonna:* my lady; *his right wits:* his true state of mind

293   *perpend:* pay attention; *give ear:* listen

299-300 *induced me . . . on:* persuaded me to put on the appearance that I did

301-302 *I/leave . . . of:* I forget the respect that I owe you.

307   *This savours . . . distraction:* This doesn't sound very much like madness.

308   *See him deliver'd:* Go and arrange his release.

309-310 *so please . . . wife:* Now that I have given further thought to these things, I hope you might be pleased to consider me as a sister as much as you wanted me as your wife.

311   *One day:* the same day; *crown the alliance on't:* serve as an occasion for two marriages, confirming our new relationship

312   *at my proper cost:* at my own expense

313   *apt:* ready; *embrace:* accept

314   *quits you:* releases you from your duties

315   *mettle:* natural disposition

316   *soft:* gentle; *breeding:* upbringing

Olivia: How now! Art thou mad?

Feste: No, madam, I do but read madness; an your ladyship
    will have it as it ought to be, you must allow Vox.   290

Olivia: Prithee, read i' thy right wits.

Feste: So I do, madonna; but to read his right wits is to
    read thus: therefore perpend, my princess, and give ear.

Olivia: Read it you sirrah.   [*To Fabian.*]

Fabian: [*Reads.*] *By the Lord, madam, you wrong me, and*   295
    the world shall know it. Though you have put me into
    darkness and given your drunken cousin rule over me, yet
    have I the benefit of my senses as well as your ladyship.
    I have your own letter that induced me to the semblance I
    put on; with the which I doubt not but to do myself much   300
    right, or you much shame. Think of me as you please. I
    leave my duty a little unthought of, and speak out of my
    injury.

                         The madly-used Malvolio.

Olivia: Did he write this?   305

Feste: Ay, madam.   He doesn't sound mad (crazy)

Duke: This savours not much of distraction.

Olivia: See him deliver'd, Fabian; bring him hither.

                            [*Exit Fabian.*]

My lord, so please you, these things further thought on,

To think me as well a sister as a wife,   310

One day shall crown the alliance on't, so please you,   Double wedding

Here at my house and at my proper cost.   Olivia will pay.

Duke: Madam, I am most apt to embrace your offer.

    [*To Viola.*] Your master quits you; and for your
    service done him,   I release you from servantness

So much against the mettle of your sex,   315

So far beneath your soft and tender breeding,

And since you call'd me master for so long,   My hand in marriage

Here is my hand. You shall from this time be

Your master's mistress.   you are the master of your master: PUN

Olivia: A sister! You are she.

    [*Re-enter Fabian with Malvolio.*]

Duke: Is this the madman?

Olivia: Ay, my lord, the same.   320

    How now, Malvolio?

322   *Notorious:* outrageous

323   *peruse:* read through carefully

324   *hand:* handwriting

325   *from it:* differently; *phrase:* style

326   *invention:* composition

327   *grant:* admit

328   *in the modesty of honour:* with proper regard for your own honour

329   *clear lights:* obvious signs

330   *Bade:* ordered

332   *lighter:* inferior

333   *acting this:* when I did this

334   *suffer'd:* allowed

336   *geck and gull:* fool and dupe

337   *invention:* trickery

339   *character:* handwriting

340   *out of question:* without a doubt

341   *bethink me:* remember

342   *camest:* you came

343   *forms:* ways

343-344   *presupposed/Upon thee:* suggested to you beforehand

345   *This practice . . . pass'd:* This trick has worked most cruelly.

346   *grounds:* motives; *authors:* creators

350   *Taint:* spoil; *condition:* situation (i.e., happiness)

354   *Upon some . . . parts:* because of some stubborn and discourteous behaviour

355   *conceived against him:* seen and resented in him; *write* wrote

356   *importance:* importunity, request

357   *In recompense whereof:* as a reward for which

Malvolio: Madam, you have done me wrong,
Notorious wrong.
Olivia: Have I, Malvolio? No.
Malvolio: Lady, you have. Pray you, peruse that letter.
You must not now deny it is your hand.
Write from it, if you can, in hand or phrase; 325
Or say 'tis not your seal, not your invention.
You can say none of this; well, grant it then,
And tell me, in the modesty of honour,
Why you have given me such clear lights of favour,
Bade me come smiling and cross-garter'd to you, 330
To put on yellow stockings and to frown
Upon Sir Toby and the lighter people;
And, acting this in an obedient hope,
Why have you suffer'd me to be imprison'd,
Kept in a dark house, visited by the priest, 335
And made the most notorious geck and gull
That e'er invention play'd on? Tell me why.
Olivia: Alas, Malvolio, this is not my writing,
Though, I confess, much like the character;
But out of question 'tis Maria's hand. 340
And now I do bethink me, it was she
First told me thou wast mad; then camest in smiling,
And in such forms which here were presupposed
Upon thee in the letter. Prithee, be content.
This practice hath most shrewdly pass'd upon thee; 345
But when we know the grounds and authors of it,
Thou shalt be both the plaintiff and the judge
Of thine own cause.
Fabian: Good madam, hear me speak.
And let no quarrel nor no brawl to come
Taint the condition of this present hour, 350
Which I have wonder'd at. In hope it shall not,
Most freely I confess, myself and Toby
Set this device against Malvolio here,
Upon some stubborn and uncourteous parts
We had conceived against him. Maria writ 355
The letter at Sir Toby's great importance;
In recompense whereof he hath married her.

[Handwritten margin notes:] About the letter from the Maria. | Coherance | Sir Toby, Maria. | Malvolio gets the punish them to. the way he wants. | Trying to confess. | Coherance | Tattle tale.

358   *sportful:* playful

359   *pluck on:* prompt, induce

360   *If that:* if; *justly:* fairly

361   *pass'd:* happened

362   *baffled:* publicly humiliated

365   *interlude:* entertainment

369   *whirligig:* spinning top

371   *notoriously abused:* shamefully mistreated

373   *of:* about

374   *convents:* calls together, is suitable

375   *combination:* marriage

379   *habits:* clothes

380   *fancy's:* love's

381   *When that I was and:* when I was only

383   *toy:* trifle

385   *came to man's estate:* grew up to become a man

389   *to wive:* to take a wife

391   *swaggering:* boasting; *thrive:* succeed

How with a sportful malice it was follow'd,
May rather pluck on laughter than revenge,
If that the injuries be justly weigh'd   360
That have on both sides pass'd. *What goes around comes around.*
Olivia: Alas, poor fool, how have they baffled thee!
Feste: Why, "some are born great, some achieve greatness,
and some have greatness thrown upon them." I was
one, sir, in this interlude, one Sir Topas, sir, but that's   365
all one. "By the Lord, fool, I am not mad." But do
you remember? "Madam, why laugh you at such a
barren rascal? An you smile not, he's gagged;" and thus
the whirligig of Time brings in his revenges.
Malvolio: I'll be revenged on the whole pack of you. *[Exit.]* 370
Olivia: He hath been most notoriously abused.
Duke: Pursue him, and entreat him to a peace.
He hath not told us of the captain yet.
When that is known and golden time convents,
A solemn combination shall be made   375
Of our dear souls. Meantime, sweet sister,
We will not part from hence. Cesario, come;
For so you shall be, while you are a man;
But when in other habits you are seen,
Orsino's mistress and his fancy's queen.   380

        [Exeunt all, but Feste.]

Feste: *When that I was and a little tiny boy,*
           With hey, ho, the wind and the rain,
        A foolish thing was but a toy,
           For the rain it raineth every day.

        But when I came to man's estate,   385
           With hey, ho, the wind and the rain,
        'Gainst knaves and thieves men shut their gate,
           For the rain it raineth every day.

        But when I came, alas! to wive,
           With hey, ho, the wind and the rain,   390
        By swaggering could I never thrive,
           For the rain it raineth every day.

233

393   *came unto my beds:* grew much older

395   *With tosspots . . . heads:* Like other drunkards, I always had
a hangover.

399   *that's all one:* that doesn't matter any more

But when I came unto my beds,
　　With hey, ho, the wind and the rain,
With tosspots still had drunken heads,　　　　　395
　　For the rain it raineth every day.

A great while ago the world begun,
　　With hey, ho, the wind and the rain,
But that's all one, our play is done,
　　And we'll strive to please you every day.　　[*Exit.*] 400

By deffinition Feste is a fool,
yet he is the only one awake
enough not to be fooled at all.

PARADOX

Act 5, Scene 1: Activities

1. Indignation, the feeling of being wronged or unjustly treated, is one of the strongest human emotions. What motivates Antonio's indignation in this scene? Would he have expected Sebastian to treat him differently? If so, why?

   a) With a partner, write out the rules of conduct and courtesy which a gentleman of Antonio's time were expected to follow. Now list the rules of today's society that reflect our values. Compare the two "codes" and consider what might account for the similarities and the differences between them.

   b) Construct a contemporary parallel to Antonio's situation by composing a creative piece which reflects the power and strength of indignation. Consider, as possibilities, a letter, a poem, a dialogue, a short scene, or a journal entry.

2. "I'll sacrifice the lamb that I do love,
   To spite a raven's heart within a dove."
   (lines 126–127)
   In this scene, Orsino is another character who feels betrayed by someone close to him. What other emotions magnify his anger to the point where he threatens to kill the one he loves? Which (if any) of his emotions are justified? How do you account for his sudden reversal of intention when he discovers that Olivia and Sebastian are married?

   As a counsellor, write a report of Orsino's conduct in which you either condemn or excuse his language and behaviour.

3. Sir Toby is another character who expresses his sense of indignation in this scene. Why does he blame his injury upon Sir Andrew? What does this reveal about him? Write a letter to Sir Toby in which you offer your advice about his personal relationships.

4. "I'll be revenged upon the whole pack of you." (line 370)
   How does Malvolio's promise introduce a "sour note"
   into the harmonious resolution of the play? How does
   it provide a touch of realism to an otherwise fanciful
   conclusion? What does this reveal to you about
   Shakespearean comedy? Consider the following ideas:
   - If you like Shakespeare's incomplete resolution of the
     play, write a brief defence of his ending, explaining
     its appeal.
   - If you would have preferred a different resolution, out-
     line a version in which Malvolio is included in the
     harmony of the happy ending.

5. Throughout the play, Feste has commented wisely upon
   the foolish behaviour of himself and others. He has
   been, indeed, a wise fool. In a group discuss your
   responses to these questions.
   - In what ways does Feste's closing song generalize
     upon the follies which he has been condemning?
   - Why might Shakespeare have ended this play with
     Feste and his song?
   - In what ways is this an appropriate ending for a
     comedy?
   Record your group's thoughts on these questions so
   that you can share them in a full-class discussion.

Consider the Whole Play

1. Now that you have finished reading *Twelfth Night*, you will probably want to discuss in small groups or as a class some of the issues and concerns upon which the play is built. Some of the main questions include:
   - What is "true love"? How is it different from other kinds of love, such as infatuation, self-love, or brotherly love?
   - What are some of the values and responsibilities of friendship?
   - What are some common social roles by which we identify and classify individuals? To what extent do you think it is fair to use these categories or stereotypes?
   - What are examples of foolishness and weakness which plague humanity? How might they be avoided?
   - What are some rules (or conventions) that people consider as they interact with others? What happens when these guidelines are too strictly observed or ignored completely?

   In your discussion, consider how your understanding of the play as well as your personal experience led you to your conclusions. Write about one of the topics above in your journal. Answer the questions with examples both from your own experience and from the play.

2. *Twelfth Night* includes many lines and images which stimulate thought. Use one of the quotations listed below as a springboard for creative writing. Before you begin, decide on a purpose for writing and on an intended audience.

   You might consider writing a short story, a fable or myth, a personal essay, a newspaper editorial, poetry, a dialogue, a short play script, or a letter.

Use your imagination!
- If music be the food of love, play on.
- Care's an enemy to life!
- Some are born great, some achieve greatness, and some have greatness thrust upon 'em.
- Love sought is good, but given unsought is better.
- Thus the whirligig of time brings in his revenges.
- Youth's a stuff will not endure.
- 'Tis but fortune, all is fortune.
- Dost thou think, because thou art virtuous, there shall be no more cakes and ale?

3. Part of the fun of *Twelfth Night* lies in the complex and intricate interweaving of different plot lines:
   - Orsino's courtship of Olivia
   - Olivia's courtship of Cesario
   - Viola's dilemmas and schemes
   - Andrew's treatment by his friends
   - Malvolio's treatment by his enemies
   - Sebastian's mistaken identity and confusion

   In small groups, list in sequence the events which comprise each plot line. Note all the incidents or events which are common to more than one plot line. Construct a chart which illustrates the interweaving of the plots. Use different colours to identify each plot.

   Display your chart to the class, explaining the purpose and the interweaving of the different colours.

4. *Twelfth Night* ends with the marriage of three couples. With a partner or in a small group, decide which of the marriages you think will be successful and which will fail. Consider the personality of each character and the reasons each has for entering into marriage.

   a) Using words or illustrations, create before-and-after portraits of the different couples. The "before" portrait should describe them on their wedding date; the "after" should describe them one year later.

b) Draw some general conclusions about good and bad reasons for getting married. Use these to compile a check-list for the use of prospective husbands or wives.

5. *Twelfth Night* seems to suggest that moderation in all aspects of life is to be preferred over excess. With a partner, identify the characters in *Twelfth Night* who act in a way that might be considered excessive or immoderate. In one or two sentences describe each character's excesses. List the various problems that result from their excessive behaviour. Discuss how a more moderate approach to life might have avoided these problems. Summarize your discussion for another pair.

6. When certain qualities of character are associated automatically with any member of a fixed group – a racial or cultural minority, a social or economic class, even a whole gender – the result is a stereotype.

a) With a partner or in a small group, list the characters in *Twelfth Night* who you think are stereotypes. What is stereotypical about them? Which stereotypes would you call negative ones? which would you call positive? Which groups are most unfairly treated by the stereotyping? Share your observations with classmates.

b) Compare the comic stereotyping in this play with the stereotyping in a modern play, film, or television series you know. Use the following headings to organize your observations:
• Group(s) Stereotyped
• Purpose(s) of the Stereotyping
• Fairness or Unfairness of the Stereotyping
• Damage or Danger to the Group(s) Stereotyped
Use your findings to lead a class discussion on stereotyping in drama and its effect on our social attitudes.

7. Like most of Shakespeare's comedies, *Twelfth Night* is filled with music and song. Using a good history of music and a record library, research the following questions:
   - What instruments would court musicians play in Shakespeare's time?
   - What instruments would be played by ordinary people?
   - What instruments were used to accompany singing?
   - What was the characteristic style of singing?

   Find recorded versions of the songs in *Twelfth Night*, or find the music and perform it yourself. Present your findings on Elizabethan music, including performances you found or your own live or taped performance. You might consider making an Elizabethan music video.

8. Northrop Frye, a noted literary critic, suggests that a typical comedy moves from an old, rigid, and "sick" society (as presented in the opening scenes) to a new, youthful, and free society (presented in the final scenes). If this pattern is a correct one, it follows that many of the major characters must undergo a change or transformation during the course of the play.

   a) With a partner or in a small group, examine the beliefs and behaviour of Olivia and Orsino in the opening scenes of the play. How do their attitudes change during the course of the play? What causes these changes? How will Illyrian society benefit from these new attitudes?

   b) As a citizen of Illyria, offer your observations on your "new" society and predict how your own life might change. Write a diary entry, a letter to a friend in another country, or a newspaper column to express your opinions.

9. Imagine that *Twelfth Night* is a new play about to be released into a very competitive entertainment market.

Using any of the media available to you (television, magazines, billboards, radio), create an advertising campaign for the play, including visuals, copy, and at least one script for a thirty-second television spot. Videotape your commercial(s) if possible. Provide a schedule or calender to explain how your campaign will unfold as opening night approaches. Perhaps your teacher might use your advertising to stimulate interest in *Twelfth Night* for next year's class!

10. The language of *Twelfth Night* includes colloquialisms and slang, particularly in the scenes with Sir Toby and his friends.

   a) With a partner, compile a glossary of Elizabethan expressions used in the text. Translate each Elizabethan expression into modern language. For example, you might translate "Go shake your ears!" as "Get lost, fool!"

   b) Create dialogue between two people in a modern setting. Use your glossary to replace the modern slang with Elizabethan slang. Prepare a dramatic reading of your script.

11. a) Malvolio's name provides a clue to his role and personality. With the help of a dictionary, unlock the secret of Malvolio's name. What other examples of word-play on characters' names can you find in *Twelfth Night* ? Share your discoveries with a partner.

   b) In a small group, brainstorm a list of other character names that work in this way, either by defining personality traits (such as *Little Mary Sunshine*, *Robin Goodfellow*, and *Wendy Darling*) or by suggesting traits (such as *Darth Vader*, *Billy Pilgrim*, and *Nurse Ratched*). Consider all types of literature, including television and film. Select three or four names for personal research. Present your discoveries in the form of a short oral report to other members of your group.

12. The roles, aspirations, and expectations of women have changed greatly since Shakespeare's time. As a way of examining these changes, set up a television talk-show with a modern feminist interviewing Shakespeare. The interviewer should prepare some challenging questions for Shakespeare based on the social inferiority of *Twelfth Night's* female characters. The student playing Shakespeare should review the remarkable strengths found in these characters to defend the presentation of women.

Role-play the interview for a group or the class (or you might videotape the interview). Remain in role to answer any questions from the audience.

With the class, discuss your ideas about how today's definition of women's role in society has changed from the definition that applied in Shakespeare's time.

13. Choose one of the following activities:

a) You are a casting director for a movie studio. You have just been assigned the task of finding the cast for a movie version of *Twelfth Night*. Prepare a list of first and second choices of actors for each role, explaining to the producer your reasons for each selection. Concentrate on why each actor is well-suited to the personality, physical appearance, and creative demands of each role.

b) You are an actor auditioning for one of the major roles in *Twelfth Night*. You want to show the producer and the director (who may be classmates, or your teacher) that you are right for the part. Choose a piece of costume or a prop that will help you look or feel the part. Now choose a speech from the play that you feel conveys the essence of the role. Prepare the speech for an audition, using the prop or costume piece and incorporating your interpretation of the character. Be prepared to explain the reasons for both your choice of prop and your choice of speech.

14. "If this were played upon a stage now, I could condemn it as an improbable fiction."
(Act 3, Scene 4, lines 124–125)
Some people complain about dramatic situations and actions which appear implausible and unrealistic. For example, how could Viola possibly be mistaken for a man so easily? How could Olivia switch her love from Viola to Sebastian without a second thought? Most people, however, accept a difference between real life and the conventions of the stage, offering a "willing suspension of disbelief" when they enter the theatre.

a) With a partner, compile a list of "improbable" events in stories which you have seen on stage or on screen or read in books. Determine which of these events you are willing to accept and which you reject. What makes you accept some events and reject others?

b) In a journal entry, reflect upon your willingness or unwillingness to accept the "improbable" events of Twelfth Night.

15. Shakespeare's comedies feature a number of characters in disguise. Viola is the obvious example in Twelfth Night. You will also find heroines disguised as young men in Shakespeare's The Merchant of Venice and As You Like It.

Read either of these plays to discover the reason for the disguise, the troubles and conflicts the disguise causes, and the contribution it makes to the final outcome of the play. Present your findings to the class in the form of an oral report.

16. In a small group, recall the "elimination" of Malvolio at the end of *Twelfth Night* and discuss your responses to the following questions:
    - Why is Malvolio unable to share in the happy ending?
    - Who is responsible for his departure?
    - What evidence indicates that the other characters will seek to include him in their society?

    Compare the fate of Malvolio to the fate of one or more of the following characters from other Shakespearean plays:
    - Shylock in *The Merchant of Venice*
    - Duke Frederick in *As You Like It*
    - Egeus in *A Midsummer Night's Dream*
    - Don John in *Much Ado About Nothing*

    Why must these characters be eliminated or overruled in the final scenes? Are there other ways in which Shakespeare might have dealt with them? Share your ideas with a partner or other members of a class. Record your conclusions in a journal entry.